Enjoy!

Percival Dodd.

Wherwell and Chilbolton:

Personal Memories and a Little History

by

Percival Irving Trodd

Editor: Wendy Andrews

Photographic retoucher: Viv Broughton

George Mann Publications

Published by
George Mann Publications
6 Malthouse Close
Easton, Winchester
Hampshire, SO21 1ES
+44(0)1962 779944

Copyright © Percival Irving Trodd 2013

All rights reserved
No part of this publication may
be reproduced, stored in a retrieval
system, or transmitted in any form or
by any means, electronic, mechanical,
photocopying, recording or otherwise
without the prior permission
of the copyright holder

A CIP catalogue record for this book
is available from the British Library

ISBN 978-1-907640-11-7

George Mann Publications

Contents

§ Introduction iii

1: Father's Early Working Life 1

2: Our Wherwell Cottage 9

3: The Priory and Estate 25

4: Wherwell Village Life 30

5: Education 74

6: The Carpenter's Shop 86

7: Duty in War and Peace 105

8: Transport 121

9: Religious and Other Groups 152

10: Chilbolton 172

11: In Celebration 188

Acknowledgements

Cover picture – The River Test (reproduced by permission of the Francis Frith Collection)

Illustrations, other than those from the author's collection, are acknowledged in the picture captions.

I am most especially grateful to my daughter Wendy for her invaluable assistance throughout the production.

I am also grateful to Ken Braxton, Viv Broughton, Brian Fakes, Peter Harding, Bill Jones, Tony King, George Mann, Henry Poore and Margaret Trowbridge for their contributions.

Introduction

This story is a tribute to my parents. It reflects on village life in Wherwell and Chilbolton, when the horse and cart were the norm, when water was dipped from the river or a well, and when paraffin lamps and candles provided the means of light. At a time when the working population were employed in the village, many at the Priory mansion and estate and lived in cottages provided.

A century ago my great aunt Sarah Child (née Tovey) living in Ivy Cottage, Wherwell, together with a little help from my father, purchased our Wherwell cottage in the Wherwell Estate Sale in 1913. It was specifically acquired for setting up my father's building business at some future date, which was in 1919 when we moved from Chilbolton to Wherwell. The cottage overlooked the river Test and rising Mount Pleasant, separated by road and railway.

Brought up in this charming village in Hampshire this records the many and varied memories of my early years.

My story starts not in Wherwell, but in Chilbolton – then just a small village a mile further east – as it was there my life began when I was just a baby during the Great War of 1914-1918.

Ilustrative maps of Wherwell and Chilbolton

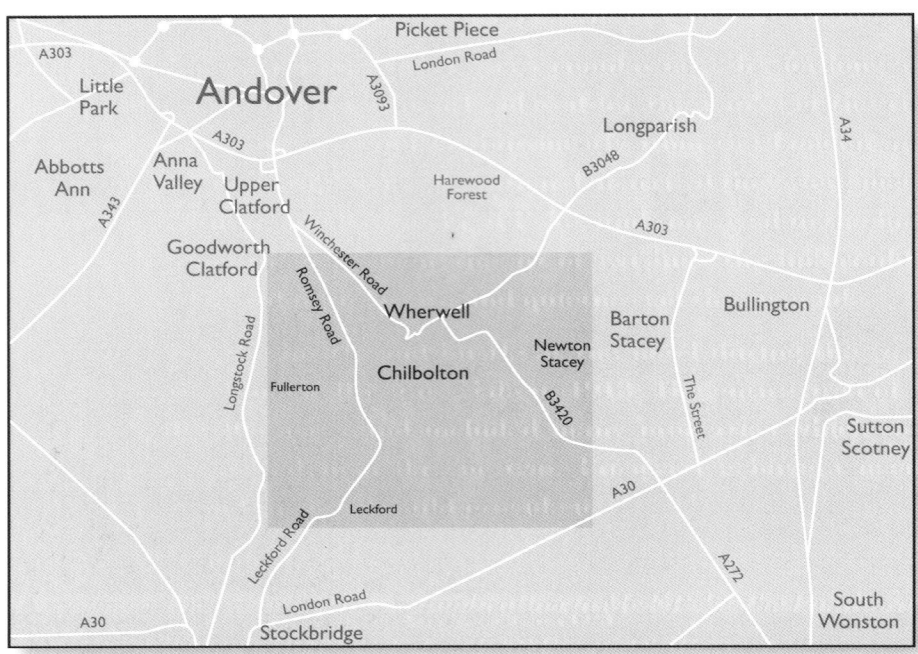

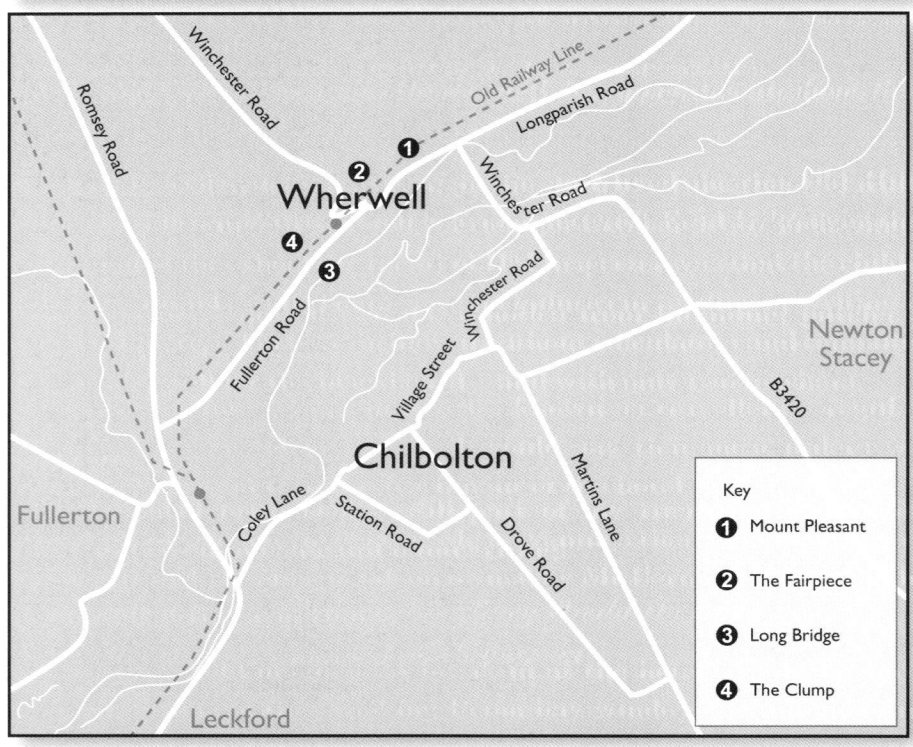

Chapter 1

Father's Early Working Life

My father, Sydney Percival Trodd, a loving family man, was a skilled carpenter, joiner and builder (as was his father before him at the family home at Plaitford), having served an apprenticeship in earlier years with one of the largest building contractors in the area — C Grace & Sons of Clatford (with a telephone number of just two digits 37). Grace & Sons was also a contractor to the War Office. Father was involved with Mr Frank Grace (son) in large construction contracts in the Tidworth area from its Ludgershall Branch, which included the Ian Hamilton Soldiers' Home in 1908. He was also involved in building the new and much larger Wesleyan Methodist Chapel at Collingbourne Kingston in 1914, which adjoined the old chapel and connected to it via a new vestry. It was described as a pleasing edifice. The cost was around £1,100 (of which £480 was contributed by a local family of stalwart Methodists). The chapel had seating for 130 people. The architect was from Caversham.

My father in the 1920s.

The Ian Hamilton Soldiers' Home in 1908 taken by father.

The Ian Hamilton Soldiers' Home as pictured in the 1980s.

Another location for father's work was Biddesden House. It was when working there that he came across an old handwritten bill underneath floorboards. He showed it to Mr Grace and suggested he keep it, but it was for father to keep and to frame. It is difficult to decipher the wording but in part it appears to read:

Greville Hobbs   His Bill 1714

For moving the door frame under the …   *One day £0 - 1 - 4*
house and other works

For moving of … and the door …   *One day £0 – 1 – 4*
against the … and other work

    £0 – 2 – 8

A piece of history which now hangs in my lobby.

Also in the early part of the Twentieth Century there was building work at Amport and further afield in the Winchester area. Closer to home at Middleton House, Longparish and Fullerton Manor – the latter a spacious red brick construction with nearby coach-house and attractive clock tower (now converted into apartments).

Fullerton Manor built in 1906 *(courtesy of Anthony Ansell)*.

Father was the last carpenter to work at Fullerton Manor, hanging the heavy doors and fitting the door furniture. (He later told me about the Roman Mosaic lifted from a nearby field close to the river Anton and re-laid in the Manor construction.)

It was when father was working on the pitched roof (no trusses then) at a new house construction at Itchen Abbas, which was close to the Winchester/Alresford/Alton railway line, that he paused to sit on a roof purlin and wave to a passing train – something we all liked to do in bygone days. Unknown to father one of the passengers was Mr C Grace, he had spotted him but did not know it was in fact Sydney Trodd. On returning to his office at Clatford he told his foreman to sack him for wasting his time. When told who it was he quickly withdrew the order. It was later that the foreman told father about it.

In those days workmen were expected to find lodgings near the building construction site and within cycling distance. Father bought his bicycle, complete with oil lamp, tyre pump and saddlebag tool kit from the Colliss Cycle Shop in Bridge Street, Andover and later acquired an acetylene (gas) lamp. Of course there were no cars then but there was a train service from Ludgershall to Tidworth.

For work at Tidworth father found lodging over Lloyds Bank, Ludgershall. His landlady had a son who later became a police sergeant at Stockbridge. For construction work at Wonston Grange and Itchen Abbas it was over a shop in Kings Worthy, whilst at Fullerton Manor it was with Mrs Brown in Wherwell. Usually he paid his landlady just a few shillings a week. It was whilst working at Fullerton Manor that he met his wife to be – my mother. His daily lunch at building sites was the top half of a cottage loaf with cheese and onion.

Before the Great War, building work tradesmen's pay for skilled carpenters was 5d per hour.

The Wedding Day

The marriage of Sydney Trodd and Gertrude Blackall was planned for 3 June 1908 in Wherwell; they would then start their married life in Amport. Mr C Grace was informed of the plans for his forthcoming marriage which meant he would not be at work that day. He also brought to his notice that 5d an hour would be inadequate to maintain a

My parent's wedding day in Wherwell with guests assembled in the paddock area of my grandparent's home in Fullerton Road.

house and living. However Mr Grace was not receptive and refused both, saying that the work which father was then doing had to be completed by a given date. This was unreasonable, especially after nearly 10 years' service. Father responded by saying – "then I will leave you". However, it had a happy ending for Mr Grace finally gave him the day off work and increased his hourly pay from 5d to 6d. There was no such thing as a honeymoon, nor pay for Bank Holidays.

The way of life was 'no work no pay'. In summertime the working day was from was 6.00 am to 6.00 pm. Saturday working was 6.00 am to noon.

Father's Service during the Great War

After 15 years' service father left Grace & Sons in May 1916 as he had been called upon for War work in the south of the county with the well-known shipbuilders Harland and Wolff Limited at Southampton Docks. He worked on the Cunard liner *RMS Aquitania*, undergoing re-conversion, and with the ship's conversion back to a hospital ship. Workmen were ferried by Tender to and from the liner when anchored in the Solent. His War work finally led him to Supermarine aviation and seaplane production, which then mainly consisted of wood. I still have his War service badge, number 86309 – a proud and treasured possession.

A little about the *RMS Aquitania*, the largest, longest serving and best known of all the Cunard liners. Her career spanned 35 years and took her through the two World Wars. At the outbreak of the Great War (after only three Atlantic crossings to New York) the ship was converted for use as an armed merchant cruiser and bristled with guns. On one of her patrols in dense fog the ship collided with another vessel, both were damaged but not in danger of sinking and *Aquitania* returned to Liverpool for repair. As a result of this incident, and after a court of inquiry, it was decided that *Aquitania* was too big for such a role and laid up until a useful role could be found for her. This came in the spring of 1915, with the Allied landings on the Gallipoli peninsula in which huge numbers of troops had to be transported. Along with the *Mauretania*, *Aquitania* was urgently required to carry three divisions of troops to the area for which 800 more berths were required. After three trooping runs to the Mediterranean, *Aquitania* was fitted out as a hospital ship and served in this role until the following January. She regularly arrived in Southampton Docks with nearly 5,000 patients and 20 ambulance trains were required to convey them to various hospitals. After undergoing engine maintenance the ship returned to Liverpool and was laid up. In April 1916 *Aquitania* was discharged from Government service altogether and ordered to Southampton, where Harland and Wolff had undertaken to recondition her for Cunard's service. In July 1916, before the work was completed, *Aquitania* was once more requisitioned by the Government and orders given to fit her out as a hospital ship once again. The hospital ship *HMHS Britannic* (White Star Line) was mined in the Aegean Sea and *Aquitania* was ordered to the Mediterranean to replace her, calling at Gibraltar to embark more nurses. Later in 1917 *Aquitania* was again laid up, this time in the Solent. The costly lesson learned earlier when the Government had paid Cunard to recondition the ship was heeded and she was left fitted out as a hospital ship, until the final reversion to troop carrying for the American Expeditionary Force which continued until the end of the War.

RMS Aquitania – from a Wills Cigarette card *(courtesy of Ken Braxton)*

Written by Mr Frank Grace on 16 May 1916 in a letter of reference for father when leaving:

> "We are pleased to say that we have always found him honest, sober and reliable and very industrious. We understand he is leaving today for Government service and wish him every success."

A fitting tribute to him (I still have the letter).

I remember mother telling me that when father was working in the joinery shop at Grace & Sons, Clatford he took every opportunity to study building plans in the office – such was his quest for building construction knowledge.

Mr A J (Jim) Dunning, a bricklayer, who also worked for C Grace & Sons, asked my father to join him in a partnership after the War, but this he declined as his desire was to be self-employed and to own a carpentry and building business.

The Way Forward

In 1916 my parents moved from Amport to a bungalow in Branksome Avenue. Our home was then the only building in that area and was surrounded by open grassland with views, though distant, of Chilbolton Common and beyond. The property is still a part of the local scene.

The bungalow was owned by an uncle (my mother's brother, Irving). He had been working at my grandparents' shop in Fullerton Road, assisting in the bakehouse and with the daily bread rounds. Together with his elder brother, Henry, they had been called up for War service and both joined the Royal Navy. Their younger brother, Frederick, later joined the Army. All three survived the War. The bungalow was provided for our living until the end of hostilities, when hopefully we would move to Wherwell. I remember it well for it had a smart white painted verandah which graced the frontage.

Father and a great aunt who was living in Wherwell had bought a cottage when the Wherwell Estate was sold in 1913 (I still have the Sale Catalogue with the purchase details written in it). The cottage had an adjacent piece of land that could serve as a builder's yard, which was accessible and level with the road. It contained a small building which in previous years had been used as a workshop. However, father's War work delayed any opportunity to move until the armistice was signed. As soon as peace was declared it was time for father's dream to become reality and the Trodd family to bid Chilbolton farewell and move into the Wherwell cottage.

Our Wherwell home at the time of purchase in 1913 as part of the Wherwell Estate sale. Frank Whitehorne was the previous occupant.

Cover page of the Wherwell Estate Sale Catalogue 1913.

I was the baby of the family and had an elder brother, Norman, who was five years old and already at the village school. Our sister, Vera, was born later, increasing our number to five – mother, father and three children.

Chapter 2

Our Wherwell Cottage

The Beginning

We occupied the cottage in 1919 but it left much to be desired, father was distraught for it was not at all acceptable for our living. There was much to be done, time was a problem, but 'where there's a will, there's a way'. His workmen would be called in when possible for it was a case of 'all hands to the pump' – as it was with the blacksmith when wheel bonding!

Frank Whitehorne, formerly head gardener at the Priory.

The small (single storey) low ceiling, lean-to front room had to be demolished. All now long gone but not forgotten for I remember sitting there on the carpet by the fireside – distanced by a heavy brass fire fender, running my first train set, just a small circle of track with engine and two carriages – a Christmas present. I also remember the small window with shutters.

Two spacious rooms were added to the cottage with a characteristic blend to match, particularly with the heavy oak timbers and moulded brackets. The first floor room with overhang and attractive oriel window gave it a pleasing period style appeal. I tried my hand at brick-laying in the early stages of construction, but was too slow for father. What I did enjoy was nailing the plaster laths to the ceiling joists. The windows (four) and all the joinery used were made in the carpenter's shop.

My home in 1922 – the front door, now with porch, moved to the opposite side of frontage.

My home (1925) now with new brickwork and windows to the roadside. Passing is Busty with Fred Young's dairy cows.

A shiny new kitchen range replaced the old iron-barred grate in the living room. For this the cavernous opening was bricked up to form a smaller opening with a shallow arch, rendered and cement faced. A new mantelshelf was added. We now had a covering plate above the flue pipe, whereas before it was an open space – with a view up the chimney!

Mother was delighted with this 'modern' improvement, heating was now controllable, especially with the oven. The range was used every day of the year for heating, cooking and hot water. Every Sunday the joint of meat was prepared and placed in the oven on a low heat before we left for morning service. Lunch was always served at one o'clock – with delicious home grown roast potatoes.

Installed by father this 'St Louis' kitchen range.

The old bread baking oven alongside was removed and in its place a fine walk-in cupboard – where we kept all our games and toys as well as mother's sewing machine. The room was now more acceptable, warmer and cleaner.

But there was more to be done. New brickwork was provided to strengthen the west wall (roadside) and this was extended up to my bedroom. A purpose built larger window was made and fitted to suit the cottage timbers; this provided more light to the room. A new south facing window was also made and fitted. In fact every window in the cottage was replaced. Also in the living room the large oak beam and floor bearing timbers were exposed, cleaned and treated. Beaver board was applied under the flooring and secured with quadrant moulding. A large hook in the main beam was probably used in bygone days for hanging bacon sides. We used it for hanging our toys – mostly model aeroplanes, then later to hang the cow bell which was found when the new larger culvert was being laid under the road to Chilbolton, where it connected with the two water meadows.

A spacious walk-in larder was formed in the kitchen/scullery area. Because of the fly problem, the meat was always protected with a muslin covered frame. The milk was also covered and boiled in hot weather. A kitchen sink was added with a semi-rotary hand-pump piped to the well in the yard. To improve access from the rear, a new opening and entrance door was provided.

To redress the sloping floor levels upstairs, the area above the kitchen/scullery was stripped out and replaced with new 8″ x 2″ timber joists and flooring – it was the only way to deal with it. A small area upstairs was partitioned off to form a bathroom – only cold water at first. A new floor was partially laid over the existing floor in my bedroom – to put me on the level! A walk-in cupboard for my clothes was formed when the old stairway was removed. I also had a new larger window with transom and fan-lights.

The family cottage at Wherwell,
left to right, Jack Pyke, Teddy Rodden, Vera Trodd, Jack Trowbridge and Norman Trodd.

Two-piece oak cabinet made by grandfather, William Trodd, in 1898 – later to grace our sitting room.

To further improve the cottage, a new hallway was formed between the new sitting room and the living room, with a new staircase and window. I now had a new cupboard under the stairs for my toys and books. Also provided was a new opening for the front door. An attractive period style new door and frame was made in the carpenter's shop. This was now accessed from a pathway enclosed with an oak paled fence and gate. I later laid this area with crazy-paving, which was surplus in the yard from a load railed to Wherwell Station. Formerly the two front entrance doorways, from different periods, were from the roadside. The old winding stairway was taken out and a passageway formed to connect the living room with the kitchen/scullery. A pedestal water closet with drainage to a cesspool in the garden completed the main improvements. Water supply was piped from a tank.

This incredible transformation gave us a most comfortable cottage home, of generous proportions with a blend of old and new. A fitting tribute to father's experience, his masterly skill and perseverance over a number of years to achieve a masterpiece.

Home with Vera in front of my summerhouse construction in 1928. The small timber building was my father's office. Note: the cylindrical galvanised water tank on the garage roof supplied piped water to the fountain.

My fountain production in 1928 – pictured is Vera and friend Willy Knapp with mother in the background.

above Norman and Vera in the garden.

left Vera and I at the garden fountain display - usually a ping-pong ball.

My home with raised roadside camber and kerb, requested by father.

The living room was the centrepiece of the home, the large oak table being the focal point for our homework, our daily chatter and play and, of course, our daily bread. We sat at table for meals, always a white linen tablecloth, which included supper with delicious ovaltine or cocoa – and a burst of the Ovaltinies song:

> *'We are the Ovaltinies, happy girls and boys,*
> *Make your request, we'll not refuse you,*
> *We are here just to amuse you,*
> *Would you like a song or story,*
> *Will you share our joys,*
> *Because we all drink Ovaltine,*
> *We are happy girls and boys'.*

If we had guests the table would be extended by adding another leaf.

After a homework session with the exercise book, it was time for board games, dominoes and jigsaws. Blow football was hilarious but exhausting. Meccano was my practical enjoyment with a horizontal stationary steam engine to drive the models - a fascinating delight. (Meccano was a construction kit of metal pieces that were bolted together to create bridges, vehicles, etc.) Using my fretwork set (which I still have) was also

above Favourite board games from our childhood days.

left Advertisements displaying Meccano and Hobbies Fretwork Outfits.

below Display of Meccano parts – one of my favourite hobbies.

a favourite, an example of this being the station footbridge and signal gantry made for the Wherwell Hornby Railway Club (see Chapter 4 – section on Activities of the Young).

A novel innovation was the magic lantern which was made of tin-plate with a curved chimney and small paraffin lamp to provide illumination for the lens. It was operated by my brother showing glass coloured slides, each consisting of five pictures. An attachment was provided for cine film and by turning a handle we had moving pictures. I particularly remember one of the films – The Ghost Train. It had been hijacked but unknown to the hijackers who were on the footplate as the train sped through the night, it was on a fast track to the sea. At the end of the line it crashed through the harbour buffers and plunged into the sea, taking all the carriages and passengers with it. It was a dreadful ending and, although it is now a long time ago, it is still implanted in my mind.

In wintertime we had a nice fire to keep us warm and a 'high-tech' Aladdin lamp, fitted with an incandescent hollow mantle which produced a brilliant white light (always placed in the centre of the table). I am pleased we did not have television then, we used our minds, our thoughts and skills to entertain ourselves. We were more active then.

Father made a shove-ha'penny board from a piece of mahogany. I was with him when he was lining it, using a sharp wood chisel. We played with old coins with a shiny copper finish, always kept in an Eucryl Toothpowder tin – and still are for I regularly enjoy a game with Wendy, my daughter.

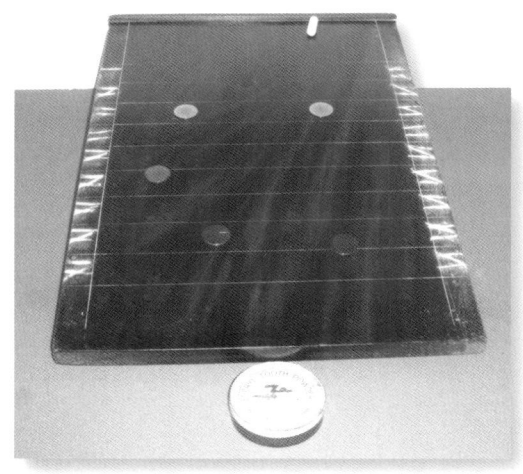

Shove-ha'penny board – now more than 80 years old.

Bedtime was strictly observed at nine o'clock, with a candle to light us to bed. I remember the bright coloured metal candlesticks with a carrying handle and a box of 'Ship' matches. Shortly afterwards mother would tuck us in, then a prayer and a verse of a favourite children's hymn before blowing out the candle.

Of course, Christmas was always exciting. On Christmas

Eve we expected Santa to fill our pillow cases with presents and good things – well, we had a big enough chimney! Perhaps for me a Hornby train set, a mechanical toy and a story book? We made our own paper chains, using selected pages from father's wallpaper pattern books – so effective. The paste was made with flour and water. A suitable Christmas tree was always found in the lower Mount. The decorations were mostly home-made with sprigs of holly and novelties. Holly was always placed over the pictures. They were truly happy times.

We also enjoyed carol singing with friends in the village. Mrs Pyke always invited us to Jack and Victor's Christmas tea party at the White Lion Hotel.

For several years we always kept a pig. Our butcher would kill it and a nearby farm worker would cut it up – rewarded with a side-of-bacon. It was then salted and hung. My mother prepared it all for the table, nothing was wasted. Apart from the tasty tender bacon, we had delicious brawn, liver and much more – including the chitterlings.

Our butcher called every Saturday evening at the back door, walked in and placed the weekly joint on the table – either beef, pork or a leg of

Copies of my favourite weekly paper 'The Modern Boy' 1928/32.

lamb with sausages; it was never wrapped. From the living room we could hear him call "butcher". Hardly anyone then knocked on the door, which was unlocked until bedtime. The joint of meat would cost about 10/- (ten shillings) or less and would usually last a week. Often it would end up in the mincing machine for a delicious cottage pie topped with potato, which we all enjoyed. The fatty pork crackling was also a favourite. There was always dripping to spare and this we sometimes ate in a sandwich. Another favourite was succulent batter pudding.

My weekly treat was a treacle tart made with delicious flaky puff pastry, also a treacle pudding. In season, we had apple tarts, plum tarts, gooseberry tarts, rhubarb tarts and much more. Mother did all the baking and cooking, including making the puff pasty. We had good food and good food meant good health.

We did not need supermarkets with sell-by dates and cooking instructions, foreign food nor Sunday trading; we had a super-mum! It was, I believe, a better way of life. There is no doubt mother would have disapproved of 24-hour opening.

With Vera at our cottage 'first gate'.

Father, his sister and her daughter at our Wherwell cottage.

A friendly chat in the village in the 1950s (my mother is on the right).

My parents at 'Mount Cottage', Wherwell in 1967 – then owned by Colonel and Mrs Dumas.

Our Wherwell cottage in wintertime.

Piano Lessons

Vera and I had piano lessons. We were fortunate to have a piano in our new sitting room – which mother often played, and was for a number of years our only source of music. It was fitted with swiveling brass candle holder brackets. During winter-time the candles provided the light but we had to endure the cold as, generally speaking, we only had a fire in the sitting room on Sundays. Our tutor, Miss Margaret Dunford from Chilbolton, never complained, I suppose she was used to it. Each lesson, every Friday evening at 6 o'clock, lasted for half an hour for which mother paid 6d (six old pennies). My sister progressed well and reached the examination grades. I still have my first piano book 'The Countryside', price 3s 0d; also my pianoforte tutor which was as far as I progressed. Miss Dunford complained because she knew I had not been putting in enough practice, particularly with the scales. She was such a nice person, probably too soft with me. To go into a cold room to practice during the evening was not helpful.

A Summer Hobby

During the summer my hobby was to get in the carpenter's shop and use father's tools; they were always left on the bench. My first attempt was the construction of a footstool, which I still use. My grandmother was so impressed

First piano book 11, 'The Countryside' which I still treasure.

left Model twin-engined aircraft made by Norman in 1932.

bottom left Model of Airship R100 with mooring mast assembled by Norman.

below Our first Kodak Vest Pocket Autographic Camera in 1932.

that I made a slightly larger one for her. She was so pleased with it that she covered it and always used it. Then I moved on to making toy boats to sail on the river, kites to fly on the Mount and then a four-wheeled 'trolley' with a steering wheel to ride in. Much of what I made was from coffin off-cuts – even then I always asked first if I could have the wood and use the tools.

They were happy days – activity suggests a life filled with good purpose, and that was my aim. In later years I made much of my own furniture.

Our First Wireless

Norman constructed our first wireless, a crystal set – it was his hobby. He bought the parts from Captain C E Dodd's wireless shop in Bridge Street, Andover for just a few shillings one afternoon on his way home from the Andover Grammar School. The cabinet was made in our carpenter's shop. In later years, possibly 1932, he bought a Marconi two-valve battery set from the same shop. Unlike the crystal set, it required a 120 volt HT (high tension) dry battery and an accumulator (wet battery) to supply low voltage to the valve filaments, the latter requiring regular recharging). Both required an aerial, and this was attached to a nearby tree – later a pole.

Things Medical

Around the turn of the twentieth century the village nurse was Mrs Ford, a widow. She lived in Yew Tree Cottage, Fullerton Road with her son Fred, who was at school with Rose Young. Her late husband was a bandmaster in the Army. No doubt she was well liked and must have delivered many babies during the time she lived there. Mrs Ford used a bicycle for transport, carrying her medical equipment in a basket on the handlebars – much the same as Rose Young did in later years when delivering milk. The cottage was close to the road and overshadowed by a large yew tree.

Later it was Mrs Smith, known to us as Nurse Smith, who lived in the cottage opposite my Wherwell home (later to be known as 'Mount Cottage'). A wooden hut, partitioned to provide two small rooms, was built in the garden area and used as a surgery for her nursing duties. This was accessed from the roadside by a pathway and entrance gate. It was an excellent facility but, as I remember, was little used. (I think Wherwell people took good care of themselves.)

Sadly her husband was struck and killed by a train at Stockbridge Station whilst crossing the line from the down platform ramp to the up platform to catch the 9.42 pm train back to Fullerton. It is quite possible the road bridge over the line and the curvature of the track prevented Mr Smith from seeing or hearing the approaching train. As a result of this tragedy a footbridge was erected over the line.

Before Nurse Smith the cottage was occupied by Mr and Mrs Joiner and used as a studio for Mr Joiner's artistry with palette and brush. He produced some fine paintings of the village which I remember seeing hanging in the cottage – more like a little museum! Mr Joiner gave one to father – it featured the blacksmith's forge and hung in our new sitting room. (It is interesting to note that the cottage is again used as an artist's studio.)

However a village nurse was not the person to carry out dentistry – that called for a journey to Andover. I had to make such a journey on the back of father's motorcycle, a Triumph two-stroke with acetylene lamp. There was no kick-start – he had to push it, run and jump on. It was a problem in wintertime. The other odd thing about it was that it had a belt drive and not a chain to the rear wheel.

Mother wrapped a warm scarf around my face for the journey. Then eight years old it was my first visit to a dentist; the problem was I had too many teeth. Mr Tutton the dentist said there were three too many and quickly pulled them out.

Most children were shy then; I do not think I said a word for it all happened so quickly. When we left he gave me some sample tubes of toothpaste and said: "You can now clean your teeth!" Generally speaking I do not think many children did clean their teeth in those days, but then we did not eat ready meals, nor chocolate and hardly any sweets, perhaps just a pennyworth a week, or every two weeks, of liquorice strips or a few aniseed balls. The old saying 'an apple a day keeps the doctor away' also included the dentist for us – and it was probably true!

If we were unwell mother would get something from a chemist or use her own remedy. In my case she would rub my chest, back and front, with camphorated oil when I was troubled with bronchitis. I wore a piece of flannel to cover it. A favourite song at the time was Auntie Maggie's Remedies sung by George Formby – but for us it was mother's remedies. *(George Formby was a popular music hall and film comedian who accompanied his singing with the ukulele.)*

Chapter 3

The Priory and Estate

Wherwell Priory and Estate

Wherwell Priory and Estate covered many acres and employed a large number of workers, all living in provided cottages. The Priory itself employed a butler, footmen, maids and cooks. Two chauffeurs were also employed, one from Rolls Royce – a bungalow was built for him near the school.

Free Milk

The Priory Estate workers were entitled to free milk. Quite often it was the children who collected it from the dairy – usually after school-time. I particularly remember Geoffrey and Tom Holloway and Ray and Adrian Parker passing our cottage en-route with their blue enamelled cans with domed lids fitted with a wire carrying handle. Bill Chant was cowman in charge of the pedigree Guernsey herd at Wherwell Priory for 42 years. He worked seven days a week and never missed a day. In recognition of this Bill was awarded the Meritorious Service Medal – so well deserved. I have memories of Bill working at the dairy, it was spotlessly kept. He produced such lovely fresh butter with a delicious taste and quality of its own. He lived in no. 2 Fair Piece Cottages.

A loyal servant for many years was Alfred John Parker. Alfred left school at the age of 12 and went to work at the Priory as a groom and handyman.

When married, Alfred and his wife Sarah lived in the Winchester Road Lodge where their two sons, Bertie and Archie (Curly) were born. Later they moved to the larger Andover Road Western Lodge, and it was here that their third child, Kathleen, was born. Doctor Loveless from Stockbridge attended and presented baby Kathleen with a newly minted half sovereign. When she was a few months old Kathleen was

Wherwell Priory Park and river Test from the Winchester Corner bridge looking south.

At the balcony casement door of Western Lodge is Sarah, wife of Alfred Parker, with her children.

photographed by Miss Marjorie Jenkins (later Lady Brecknock) who had become the proud owner of a camera.

Alfred Parker served throughout the Great War (see chapter 8) and returned to work at the Priory in 1919. Alfred was then made a chauffeur to the Lady of the Manor; he was also an electrician. Using the Priory Wolseley shooting brake (which was almost as large as the Rolls Royce) Alfred was expected to drive Colonel and Mrs Jenkins to their Scottish residence in a day – no mean feat then!

Three further moves in the village were to follow – Westmill Cottages, Fullerton Road; no. 2 of the newly built semi-detached 'Fairpiece' houses and finally to no. 1 of the terraced cottages in the High Street.

A little about the features of the Swiss chalet style Western Lodge - an impressive property with overhanging roof line, which extended over the shallow ornate bay windows. A prominent exterior feature was the substantial timber built balconies which graced both end walls, accessed independently by stairways from the Lodge frontage, providing entrance at that level. Attractively moulded handrails and 'Barley Twist' pattern spindles enhanced the overall appearance.

Set back from the road, in line and proximity with the Lodge, the massive ball-topped overhanging masonry capped piers, with heavy iron gate and frontage railings, presented a fine entrance to the main carriage-drive to the Priory Mansion from Wherwell Village Street.

It was the duty of the gate-keeper to open and close the gate when requested, the balconies provided good vision for this in both directions, in addition to providing a rapid response. The Rolls Royce chauffeur would sound the bulbous car horn by depressing it (I was there on one occasion to hear it) and no doubt before that the driver of a horse and carriage would blow his horn.

Colonel Jenkins' handsome white horses at the park railings in Wherwell High Street.

Wherwell football club players in the 1920s in the Priory Park.

The Priory shocks the cricket club, circa 1870

Around the 1870s cricket was played in the Priory Park. On 1 January 1888 Captain Montague shocked the club by withdrawing permission for the use of the park. The club held a crisis meeting at the White Lion at which Mr Scamell offered the use of a piece of ground near Fullerton Station, which was converted at a cost of £7.7s.0d. Captain Montague forwarded money to cover this cost to the secretary of the club.

It was an excellent ground in a pleasant location and when I was a boy I, with many of the villagers, would catch the evening train from Wherwell Station. It was then through the station fence at Fullerton and onto the ground.

During its long history Wherwell Cricket Club had won outright the Village Cricket Challenge Cup (Andover District) for the years 1892, 1893 and 1894. My great uncle, James Tovey, was honorary secretary during those years – he was a keen cricketer and loved his bat. His name is engraved on the Silver Challenge Cup, proudly displayed in a picture of the cricket club. A beautifully inscribed gold pocket watch was presented to him by the club.

above Wherwell Cricket Club Team 1892/94.

left Wherwell Cricket Club Team Cup – one shield bears my great uncle's name. *(courtesy of Alan Rowles)*

below Gold pocket watch presented to great uncle James Tovey by Wherwell Cricket Club.

Chapter 4

Wherwell Village Life

Life in the Twentieth Century

For most villagers life was so very different in the early years, and beyond, of the twentieth century; there was no sanitation, no bathroom, no taps to turn on and no electric light. For some, water was drawn from a well, or a shared well, for which a windlass was provided. For others it was from a hand pump, usually outside the cottages, while for those living near the river it was dipped from the river by bucket or pail – for which a concrete 'dipping step' was provided.

The lavatory (then known as a 'privy') was a sanitary pail with nearby earth box in a small wooden enclosure in the garden area or behind the wood shed. (A hole in the garden was the normal practice for disposal.) Lavatory paper was cut in squares from the daily broadsheet newspaper – common practice in those days. Elderly people used a commode, normally kept in the bedroom. The word 'toilet' was not then used.

By tradition Monday was always washing day, with an early start. Filling the copper and lighting the fire underneath it, then to get it up to boiling point was so time consuming, in fact it was hard work. Fortunately we had plenty of wood. I am sure that clothes in those days were much heavier, particularly with sheets – probably because of the colder weather we then experienced. My mother used a 'dibbing' stick to stir the clothes – I had a go but it was a bit of a struggle! The heavy solid black irons were used for ironing and always kept on the kitchen range hob.

A galvanised bath (hanging outside the lean-to woodshed) was used by the fire for the weekly 'scrub'. Such was the way of life in bygone days.

But the people of Wherwell were very much self-sufficient and most had an allotment at what we called the 'Severals' in Longparish Road (now Wherwell Playing Fields/Sports Ground). They walked by our cottage with a spade over their shoulder or tied to their bicycle and would be hard at work digging, planting and sowing. There was keen competition to grow the best crop of potatoes, cabbages, parsnips and beans. There was always plenty of rhubarb. Sweet peas were a speciality and gave colour to the scene. Children were expected to be there helping as well as playing. Mother had a plot; my sister and I would be there to help, eating delicious peas in the process.

There was plenty of fruit in the village. My grandparents and great aunt had apple, pear and plum trees as well as soft fruit. There were walnut, filbert and hazelnut trees too.

From the early twenties the head waterkeeper lived in the nearby Andover Road Priory Lodge, often (when in season) he would toss a sack containing several eels over our fence. My father skinned them and put them in a bath of water, after which they were cut into short lengths and cooked (mostly boiled). They were delicious.

The eels were trapped in large eel pods *(a type of basket)* at the weir, just a few yards up river from our cottage. They were put into special containers and on occasions my father would take these to the station in his Ford lorry to catch the early 'up' train. An amusing incident occurred at Whitchurch station in 1928 which was reported in the Andover Advertiser.

While a container was being transferred to the London train it broke open. For some minutes there was a frantic scramble by porters and passengers to retrieve the slippery contents. The eels had rapidly spread themselves over the platform and railway lines, much to everyone's amusement. It was alleged that more than one of the eels found its way into the carriages.

A travelling fish and chip van, complete with fryer, its stove pipe chimney seen above the roof line, regularly called in the village every Friday evening at 6 o'clock. For Vera and I it stopped at the blacksmith's shop and if we had a penny to spare would buy a tapered greaseproof bag full of chips. We had never tasted chips like this before. The owner of the travelling business was G Rusher from Ludgershall. It operated with a driver and server – probably a man and wife team. It came to an end with the arrival of a regular bus service.

Before the War a Walls Ice Cream vendor with his box type tricycle pedalled his way through the village once a week - usually on Sundays – displaying the 'Stop Me and Buy One' slogan with wafer ice creams at 2d and choc ices at 6d.

Among popular pastimes for the village children was the joy of rolling a hoop. For girls it was the larger wooden variety rolled with a stick, and for boys the smaller iron hoop 'trundled' along the road with a hooked-end short metal rod, to which I added a wooden handle for comfort and control. The blacksmith was on hand to repair a broken joint. The game of marbles was often played in the village street, and keenly contested. Much coveted was the larger variegated coloured marbles – known as glass 'allies' which we would often exchange (I still have some). Hopscotch was enjoyed by all, and this too was often played in the road. Skipping ropes with fancy shaped wooden handles (for some) delighted the girls – with plenty of exercise. Autumn was the time for 'conkers' – played with horse-chestnuts.

A challenging little wooden toy was a spinning top, pear-shaped with a pointed end, and sometimes steel capped. A sharp pull of the length of string, wound tightly around it, would set it spinning along the road, followed by a whipping action with the string to keep it spinning. But for some boys it was just too much of a challenge to grasp the 'knack' of the action.

Another pleasure for Vera and I was riding a little wooden scooter with spoked wheels (seen in an earlier picture). Hardly any children then had the luxury of a new bicycle. When I started work I rode mother's Hercules cycle.

I always envied the boys who could whistle – and whistle a song (as Bing Crosby used to do) for as much as I tried I just could not master the art.

The hollow elm tree – a favourite trysting place for the village lads, including me.

'Brummer', the Young Family, and Others

At the far end of the allotments in Longparish Road was a smallholding which extended north to Dublin Farm. It was worked by Mr Willshire who lived with his wife and son in Toll Cottage at Winchester Corner. Apart from growing all varieties of vegetables and soft fruit, he also had an orchard. In addition Mr Willshire was a bee-keeper and kept several hives. I have memories of seeing him at the hives using his bellows – suitably protected of course and for me unapproachable! Rhubarb cultivation was his speciality. Every Friday he used his horse and four-wheeled open cart, kept in a wooden shed with adjoining stable, near his entrance gate, to convey and sell his produce at Andover Market. Mrs Willshire was always at his side for the journey, which would take about one hour. He was popularly known as 'Brummer' Willshire, but I do not know why.

I remember him applying the brakes and stopping outside our cottage. He had brought a little blue doll's pram for my sister. It was a Christmas present that mother had bought from Parsons and Hart in Andover.

Fred Young's smallholding was mainly centred around Gavel Barn, on the corner of Mill Lane. A stable and dairy were sited here on a piece of land given to the Young family by Mrs Jenkins of The Priory.

Rose Young (Fred's sister) became the village 'milk delivery' girl. She delivered our daily milk for a number of years. She rode her bicycle with two cans slung over the handlebars, each holding three gallons of milk. A dipper measuring one pint was used to fill her customers' jugs. Mother would put two jugs on a shelf at the porch, covering them with muslin. We needed 1.5 pints. It took Rose two hours each day to complete the round, which she started at 7.00 am.

Fred Young had five cows and their pastureland was in Winchester Road, roughly between the two bridges. They passed our cottage twice a day, returning to the dairy for milking about 3.00 pm. At election times, when walking the cows back from the pasture to the dairy, Rose would say, "These are Liberal cows, vote Liberal". She had a cheery, smiling and happy personality.

Sometimes, after school, I would be sent to the dairy with a jug for an extra pint of milk and if milking was unfinished I would wait and watch the process. The milk was still warm when poured into my jug. If I also wanted eggs, Fred would say to me 'go and look for 'em', and this I enjoyed doing. His favourite name for me was 'Willum' (well that is what it sounded like) but I do not know why, but then Fred was popularly known as 'Digger'.

Having taken over his father's smallholding and dairy, Fred Young started his own haulage business with just one horse – and ended with six. They were fine animals. He employed men from the village who were strong, rugged and did sterling work.

Father often hired a horse and cart for hauling gravel from our yard pit at Chilbolton to his building sites. Busty Alexander, one of Fred's men, would be in charge. There was an abundance of clean white gravel in our yard pit that was ideal for concrete. With so many extractions it filled with water during the winter and flooded the area.

Another aspect of Fred's haulage business was with road resurfacing work. Drawn from Wherwell Station, the stone chippings were unloaded directly over the hot tarred surface by swinging the shovel in a wide arc for maximum coverage. Up to four carts (each with two men) were required for this work – necessary to coordinate it with the tarring process. Drawn off from the tar boiler (tap provided) a bucket was used to pour the boiling hot tar over the road surface. Finally the steam-roller would follow up as the work progressed. The driver was Ernie Budd, a Wherwell man. The family lived in the Court. (To avoid closure, resurfacing was restricted to half the width of the road.) I always enjoyed watching the work in progress, in particularly the steam-roller which so fascinated me.

Names I well remember from Fred Young's loyal team of workmen were Busty Alexander, and Tom and Jim Sandon. They all lived in the village. It was demanding work, especially in hot weather for they were on the move all the time.

In earlier years gravel was used for resurfacing.

Fred Young was also a coal merchant and served many of the villagers in Wherwell and Chilbolton. Delivery was always done on Saturday mornings. Busty was usually in charge. I remember the cart outside our cottage with the price tab of 1s 11d per hundredweight of coal. The price later increased to 2s 2d. The coal was always carried to the buyer's coal shed.

Wood was also used as fuel. My great aunt Sarah Child would regularly buy a sack of logs, usually silver birch. I would split them for her using a bill-hook. The logs came from Taylor's saw mill and were delivered by Fred Pyke.

Fred Pyke was also a coal merchant and used a Model 'T' Ford lorry for delivery – rather faster than Fred Young's horse and cart. His coal yard was in Fullerton Road, opposite the White Lion entrance. Busty did part-time work for him.

In earlier years Andrew Baker was the village's carrier/haulier at Gavel Barn. He employed five men from the village and in 1885 they were kept busy carting material from Wherwell Station, which had opened to traffic in June of that year. He also carted material for the new bridge being constructed in Winchester Road, which we called Big Bridge (near the Chilbolton turning) which opened for traffic on 6 November 1981.

He delivered the hazel faggots *(bundles of sticks used for fuel)* to my grandparents, used for fueling the bakehouse oven. An average delivery consisted of 15-20 faggots.

Andrew Baker and his wife at their home 'Gavelacre' in Wherwell High Street 1905 – a porch was added later by my father.

Andrew Baker was an astute businessman and kept meticulous records of every transaction from 1885 to 1916 – 31 years. He was a big man with a large family, the father of eleven children, although only two survived into adulthood. His second wife was one of my great aunts (seen in the 1905 village picture). He was an ardent member of the Primitive Methodist Chapel and a lay preacher.

Another enterprising Wherwell man in the early part of the twentieth century was George Mansbridge who lived at no. 1 Freelands Cottages in Fullerton Road. I am not sure what George did at 'Freelands' but he was also a skilled cycle repairer. For this work he used a small wooden shed in his garden and kept a supply of spare parts, including wheels, axles, ball-bearings, spokes, chains, pedals and much more.

I have memories of going there in my youth for cycle parts. Interesting for me was to watch him true-up a wheel – wobbly wheels were common in those days.

The Village Policeman

In my schooldays the village policeman for Wherwell and Chilbolton was Police Constable Barnes. He was of stout build with a somewhat serious manner and lived at no. 6 Fair Piece. He had two sons, Ernest (known as 'Chubby') and George. They were both at school with me. His wife regularly visited our cottage for a cup of tea and a chat with mother.

His practice was to push his bicycle through the village. As children we were afraid of him – expecting to be told we had done something wrong! Most children then were shy and of good behaviour. In cold and wet weather he always wore a cape, which was fastened at the neck with a hook, so smart and so protective.

The 'Milestone Inspectors' – Tramps

Tramps, described as 'milestone inspectors', regularly passed through the village on their way from Andover Workhouse to Winchester, and some regularly called at our cottage back door to beg – hot water for their billy-can, a spoonful of sugar and tea (no teabags then), also bread and milk. Some would say "thank you Ma'm" and some would say "can you spare a copper?". I do not think mother ever refused them – probably that is why they kept calling! They were also regular callers at the blacksmith's shop – probably for a warm-up.

What we called the tramps' resting place was in the woodside beyond Newton Stacey crossroads, where there was a bubbling spring of pure water to refresh them and a place to light a fire.

The handsome seven – smartly dressed Wherwell village lads (before my time).

Hawkers

Gypsy women would hawk their wares from time to time carrying a wicker basket containing clothes pegs, saucepan lids and a variety of small brushes.

There were other hawkers selling floor polishes, scrubbing brushes, shoe brushes, laces, razor blades and much more. Most items were priced in pence.

A Forced Landing

Flying from RAF Aerodrome, Andover in the late twenties a Royal Air Force Vickers Virginia twin-engined bomber (the largest then flying) made a forced landing in the field beyond Windwhistle in the direction of Wherwell. The cause of failure was quickly attended to and the heavy machine took off, slowly gaining height and narrowly missing the line of beech trees across the top ridge of the Fair Piece.

A squadron of Virginias was based at RAF Andover for a number of years, they were still flying in 1936/37 at both Andover and Worthy Down aerodromes and replaced by the more progressive Handley Page Heyford machines (though not at Andover). In 1938 development quickened with all-metal monoplane construction hastened by the onset of war.

The daily bread round in the early twentieth century –
seen here is one of Henry Blackall's horse-drawn delivery carts (Uncle Irving is holding the reins).

For nearly 30 years the premises of my grandparents' village shop and bakery business in Fullerton Road.

Shops

There were then two grocers and bakers shops in Wherwell. My grandparents owned the shop and bakery business in Fullerton Road. Freshly baked bread was delivered daily to an area that included Chilbolton, Newton Stacey, Fullerton and Longstock. Two horse-drawn bakers' carts were used for this. On Saturdays it was early evening before they arrived back. Apart from our daily bread, they also baked delicious dough cakes. I have no doubt that much of the food for Christmas treats came from the bakehouse.

The small shop window was usually filled with sweets for the children and would include aniseed balls, gobstoppers, liquorice strips and sherbet. I remember we would stand there gazing in the window – what would we buy with our hard earned halfpenny or penny? It was usually by running an errand or chopping firewood that one earned pocket money. I do not remember Easter eggs in those days – they were not then a part of Easter.

To the left of the shop was a large window which displayed hardware – brushes, buckets, galvanised baths, bowls; scrubbing brushes were commonly used then. At Christmas-time it was toys.

The small triangular piece of land at the lower end of the Old Hill was owned by my grandparents at the Fullerton Road shop. It was on this piece of land that they tethered their horses for grazing. It was a favourite place for children to play – they called it 'Black's Meadow'. It is now used by the Home Guard Club.

By today's standards people were poor, very poor, we only bought one item of what we required, never two or three – or expect to get one free! There was no money to be had from the State, it had to be earned. (The old age pension was then 10 shillings per week, payable at age 70.)

When my grandparents retired at the end of that decade they moved to Malt Cottage opposite.

Mr and Mrs Alfred Olliff kept the shop in the High Street, this included the post office which was very small and had a separate entrance. Their baker was Mr Hams who lived in what was Mr Tovey's cottage, but in earlier days he lived at no. 2 Freelands Cottages, Fullerton Road. The Twentieth Century Stores and public bar was previously run by Alfred's father, Henry Olliff. In his time he would cure and cook delicious hams to sell over the counter, something which was not continued when his son took over.

Alfred Olliff later bought a new Morris van for the daily delivery, 'Teeny' Horn was the driver. I would wait for him to arrive at the blacksmiths (8.00 am) and then go with him to Dublin Farm, hoping he would let me drive part of the way. This I did sometimes between stops, whilst he was delivering. Dublin Farm was as far as he went. Bread was not wrapped in those days, dough cakes were wrapped in greaseproof paper.

When I was 14 and still at school, Mrs Olliff asked me to work for her on Saturdays. It was always a busy day in the shop, she required an assistant and I was pleased to say 'yes'. This was an opportunity for me to learn about shop-keeping and hopefully to serve behind the counter, wearing a smart white apron – like the carpenters. Now that did appeal to me, it would surprise the customers.

From a 1906 postcard Mr Olliff (senior) at the Twentieth Century Stores with the Wherwell carrier approaching.

To start with it was mornings only 9.00 am to 1.00 pm, but quickly extended to all day working, for there was much to do. In those days my pay for working Saturday morning was 9d and for all day 1/6d.

My first job in the morning was the workmen's bar which adjoined the shop. To collect all the dirty, smelly beer mugs from the round metal tables and wash them in a bowl of hot soapy water which Mrs Olliff would place on the bar counter (no piped water then). Then there were the ashtrays to clean and wash together with the table tops. Finally, a tea towel was provided to dry the mugs with a sparkling lustre – the best part of it, for I disliked doing both. As a result of this task I have never bought a pint of beer or a packet of cigarettes.

The beer was supplied by Simmonds Brewery, the price of a pint then was just a few pence. Cigarettes were 2d for a packet of five Woodbines and 1/- (one shilling) for a packet of 10 Players.

But I did enjoy working in the shop, particularly bagging up granulated sugar and other dry goods. Using the traditional blue sugar bags I became quite adept and fast in folding and tucking in the flap. Mrs Olliff was most particular and precise in her ways and this was for me to follow. Sometimes she would stand over me with a watchful eye to check that I never measured a grain of sugar over weight, the scales had just to reach balance. Sugar was kept in bulk in one hundredweight jute sacks under the counter, with two brass scoops for ½lb and 1lb measures.

Cube sugar, in bulk, was kept in the dry goods stockroom over the rear part of the shop. It was accessed externally by a flight of stairs with a small covered landing. I would bring it down to the shop in required quantities and bag it up in similar measures. Both granulated and cube sugar were then stacked under the counter with a section for each.

On the main sales counter were two sets of attractive polished brass scales with handle-shaped brass weights – a joy to handle.

Biscuits were stocked in the traditional square shaped tins 9″ x 9″ x 9″ and stacked in front of the counter – either Kemps, slightly cheaper, or Crawfords, the more expensive; these averaged 10d to 1/3d a pound. Lyons cakes were stocked and displayed from their own metal stand, mostly swiss rolls selling at 1/-

Attractive brass weights used with Balance Scales at the Twentieth Century Stores. *(courtesy of Mrs Rosemary Barrett)*

(one shilling). Very few sweets were stocked as there was no window to display them. Rowntrees gums and pastilles were kept behind the counter but visible.

Below the shop was a spacious cellar, it was cold and dark in winter and cool in summer. The entrance was from outside the shop frontage and through a hinged trap door with a steep flight of brick formed steps with wood bearers designed to skid down beer barrels. Here we stocked a variety of tinned goods, including Fray Bentos corned beef which nearly everyone bought in those days; Skippers and Marie Elizabeth sardines, pilchards and salmon were also popular. In addition there was Nestlé skimmed milk and cream. I was expected to keep the shop shelves full and this kept me busy.

The marble topped counter at the back of the shop, at right-angles with the main mahogany customer counter, was partially screened from view with displays. This was used for dispensing butter, cheese and bacon.

First, butter was stocked in a large cube shaped block of some 12-14 inches square, wrapped in special greaseproof paper. When opened the aroma was delightful and so too was the taste. It was cut with a knife to the customer's requirement, mostly of ½lb and 1lb blocks – the most popular was 1lb. Such was the art in skilful cutting that only a dab was added to bring the scales to balance.

Next was cheese, this was stocked in a round block of 12-14 inches in diameter and of similar height. It was covered in a type of cheesecloth (similar to that of muslin) and cut with a cheese wire (a length of special wire with a small round shaped handle at each end). It was always cut in the traditional wedge shape – so simple and so easy. That too was delightful.

Finally, the smart red coloured, hand operated bacon slicing machine, which for me was 'out of bounds'. I enjoyed watching Mrs Olliff slicing off the rashers from a side of bacon, they were handled onto a sheet of greaseproof paper (which I would cut into squares from large sheets) and then dropped on the special platform scales using flat rounded weights. The smell of freshly cut bacon was also delightful and so was the taste for it was a joy to eat.

Prices then for butter, cheese and streaky rashers was 10d per lb. For back rashers it was 1/3d per lb. The most popular was streaky bacon. There was a benefit for customers in that it was always freshly cut.

During the morning I would collect order books from customers in the village and later deliver the goods, for which most would pay me. At 2.00 pm Mrs Olliff would call me to the bakehouse and remove dough cakes (still warm) from the oven, wrap them in greaseproof paper, write the customer's name on each and place them in a bread basket for me to deliver in Wherwell and Chilbolton. For this I used Mr Olliff senior's bicycle. I remember it well for the narrow handlebars and that I could scarcely reach the pedals. Not an easy bicycle for me to ride, I fell off twice when cycling across the Common on my way to Drove Road, Chilbolton – scattering the dough cakes among the many cow pats, but fortunately not in them!

I remember father hiring a horse and trap from the Twentieth Century Stores for a family outing (before the arrival of the motor car.) Entranced from an iron step at the rear we sat facing inwards – with happy chatter along the way. Father was familiar with the reins as his parents owned a horse and trap, used for business and journeys to Romsey. Refreshments for the picnic were bought from the shop and included lemonade, then in bottles with a glass marble stopper – we loved to rattle (my, that is going back a long way). It was a lovely way to travel – so peaceful, so relaxing. The Twentieth Century Stores was then run by Mr Olliff senior (Henry). The horse and trap was kept at Chilbolton where he lived. (See display sign for horse and trap hire in picture).

After Mr and Mrs Olliff retired, the shop was acquired by Robert (Bob) Hunt. He requested Mr Hams (the long serving baker with Mr Olliff) to instruct him in the art of dough making and baking, but for Mr Hams his good will was short lived as Robert Hunt thereafter dismissed him. Unable to find work in the village Mr Hams and his family moved to Stoke, where once again he worked his trade at the local shop. Mr Hams' daughter, Lilian, is still living there and I regularly keep in contact with her.

The traditional village shop has since ceased to exist at Wherwell, it is now a thriving business by William Stewart Hair Design.

Before the Second Great War, particularly in the twenties, Sunday was always peaceful, the pace of life relaxed, the anvils silent, as was the carpenter's shop with its yard gates closed and padlocked. The cordwainer and the village shops were also silent.

The bells in the steeple peeled out a call to worship for both morning and evening services at 11.00 am and 6.00 pm. Usually the peel consisted of three bells, but I have memories of the full set of five bells peeling a lovely outburst of sound, especially for Easter and during Christmas week. Busty was one of the ringers, so too were Ted Nutley and Jack Horn. Fred Goddard was for many years a church warden, he also tolled the minute bell from the church nave. Fred was a true and faithful stalwart and a good friend.

Mrs Mathie and her son outside their cottage home in Wherwell High Street – a regular visitor to the Twentieth Century Stores.

Most people then either attended church or chapel, and of course everyone walked, including those attending from Chilbolton, Cottonworth and Fullerton. From Chilbolton I particularly remember Bob Waite for his fine tenor voice, Mary Morris and Mr Tucker. All regularly attended services at the Wesleyan Methodist Chapel. In the summertime many enjoyed a favourite walk after evening worship, as I did myself. I mention this in my poem 'Memories of a Favourite Walk'.

Another enterprising character was Roland Hawkins who lived at the lower end of Church Street, often then called Lower Street. Apart from his thatching work he was also a carrier with a pony and cart. For a while he became a fishmonger and collected his supplies from Fullerton Station. A handcart was used to carry the fish around the village, but it was not a profitable venture. He also kept bees and a pig. Saturday morning was traditionally the time for killing, and I could often hear the pig squealing – not pleasant.

For a short while the shop at the north side of Pound Tree Green was used as a fruit shop. I can remember the window filled with fruit, in particular oranges which at that time were not generally available. A china shop was another venture in the village which was short lived.

Another short lived shop was a wooden building sited in Mr Pyke's meadow, entranced by wooden steps from the roadside. It was owned by a Mr Ockenden who sold household goods. At Christmas-time he also sold toys and I remember mother buying me a German-made red clockwork lorry with a starting handle to wind it up – which was unusual. Made of tin-plate it was an excellent toy (no plastic in those days).

I believe my great aunt's husband, Robert Child, a carpenter and joiner had some part in building the impressive church porch at Wherwell. He loved to talk about village life. One of our walks, when I was just a small boy, would take us to Dublin Farm and beyond to the weir which, with the river area around it, he called the Isle of Wight. Close by there was an old railway carriage which was probably used by the fishermen. There was another railway carriage further up the road at Harewood which was then occupied.

It is believed that the name Wherwell is derived from 'weir' and from 'well' as one was situated near the weir – hence you have Weir-well or Wherwell. In those days almost all the villagers had a 'well'.

A Memorable Gale

On the night of 12 January 1930 a ferocious gale uprooted many huge trees of elm, sycamore, chestnut and beech, completely blocking roads in and out of the village. Many fell in the Priory Park and probably a dozen or more in the park area around and near our cottage. On the bank at the opposite side of the road a massive elm fell across the road crashing in the park and narrowly missing our yard. It was a scene of devastation and so frightening. The telegraph wires (of which there were then two) were also brought down.

Petrol engine saws were used to cut through the huge trunks – up to four feet in diameter, in lengths of about 15 feet or less. Using skid poles each length was hauled up by tractors – one at each end, onto the waiting timber carriages (not seen today) and hauled away, some through the park to exit at the Lodge gate. It took several weeks for it all to be cut up and cleared away, after which the gaping holes left behind were filled and levelled. Loading the timber carriages was the fascinating part which captivated me. The name 'Twin City' on the tractors has stayed with me all through the years and in my mind I can still see them at work.

The metal tractor wheels were fitted with angled skewed metal plates to provide traction. A sycamore tree, close to the carpenter's shop escaped the onslaught – much to father's displeasure.

Another reason to remember the gale – riding his Triumph motorcycle, father had gone to visit his sick parents living near Romsey. The gale developed as he returned home; first the light from the gas lamp had blown out, then his cap and scarf had blown away. There was worse to come for he encountered fallen trees which blocked the road; to overcome this he laid the motorcycle on the road and pushed it underneath, then to crawl under himself and drag it clear – all in the dark and this made it a dreadful experience not knowing when the next one would fall. Father finally arrived home shaken and distressed, mother was so relieved.

The Post Office

There were, over time, three different locations for the village post office. The first was the thatched cottage next to the Twentieth Century Stores which was run by my uncle, Harry Blackall and his wife, then living in the cottage. I would often go there for mother or father. It was not only a post office as they also sold stationery and tobacco. The counter fascinated me with its display of goods. The shelves behind were stacked with an array of cigarette and tobacco packets and matches. Cigarette prices started at 2d for a packet of five Wills Woodbine. Some were 4d or 6d for a packet of 10, and 11½d for a packet of 20. Father smoked Players cigarettes. When he sent me to buy them he would give me the ½d change, which I would take to my grandparents' shop to buy a stick of liquorice or four aniseed balls. Each packet of cigarettes contained a picture card – known to us as 'fag' cards. Collecting cigarette cards was an interesting pastime, especially to achieve a full set of 40 cards. Each card was numbered and storied on the reverse side. If we had two of a kind we would swap with each other, and when passing men in the village street would ask "any fag cards Mister?" Some of the picture contents I remember were birds, animals, motor cars, railway locomotives and ocean liners.

Postage stamps cost 1d for postcards and 1½d for letters. In those days urgent communication was done by telegram.

Later Mr and Mrs Louis Chadwick and family occupied the cottage. Sadly Mr Chadwick died as a result of rat poisoning when working at The Priory.

The post office then located to the Twentieth Century Stores. A small part at the front of the shop was partitioned off for this and a separate narrow entrance doorway provided, which adjoined the shop door. The counter now extended into the post office area and this was managed by Mrs Olliff. The postbox was moved to this shop.

When I was working at the shop Mrs Olliff would clear the postbox at 5.00 pm, the mail was put in a GPO sack, sealed, and then carried over the shoulder to the station and put on the 5.32 pm down train.

The third move was to Fullerton Road where the end room (facing road) of Mr George (Doss) Spratt's bungalow was converted by father to form a post office. This entailed making and fitting a shop window, adding a new side entrance doorway with porch and providing a counter and shelving for stock. Mrs Spratt was the postmistress and Mr Spratt delivered the mail with the daily papers. Because this was situated away from the village centre, an additional postbox was provided at the entrance to New Barn Lane, the brickwork being partially recessed into the bank. This was built by father. A Sunday collection was now provided and this was at 4.00 pm.

The White Lion Hotel – 'In the Strong Country'

In my school days the White Lion had hotel status and was known as The White Lion Hotel, providing comfortable accommodation with excellent cuisine. The upper floor provided seven bedrooms for paying guests – all with fireplaces. The attractive and well stocked bar was a magnet for its clientele – though not for the village labourers and farm workers! The cellarage space was under the bar and Smoking Room; the hatchway was in the yard. Lighting was by oil lamps and in later years I remember Mrs Pyke with an Aladdin mantle lamp. A large storage tank in the yard contained paraffin with a draw-off tap. The wood shed was the end part of the thatched building at right angles with the hotel. Faggots provided the kindling wood with a bill-hook for chopping, which I often did for lighting the Club Room fire.

The large thatched building bordering the yard formed a motor and carriage house for Mr Pyke's two conveyances, one with attractive landaulet style bodywork and the other an open Tourer. In earlier years it provided stabling for eight horses. Behind it was a large vegetable garden with fruit trees, which extended to the boundary with 'Southcroft' owned by Tom Spratt. In season it provided much of the hotel's daily needs. (It is more than likely that my grandparents supplied bread and much more from their bakery and grocery shop in Fullerton Road.)

During the fishing season the hotel was a popular hostelry for long-stay wealthy fishermen, and conveniently placed for the banks of the river Test. They came from near and far but mostly from the London area, they travelled by train to Wherwell Station. On arrival they were met on the platform by their genial host, Fred Pyke, and conveyed to the hotel. I enjoyed watching the fishermen, the art of swishing the link could be clearly seen and heard in the peace and quietness of the riverside.

One can imagine the hustle and bustle at the hotel during the weeks leading up to the Wherwell Estate Sale in 1913. The entire area of the Estate covered 4,405 acres and included many properties which could not possibly be viewed in a day or two. Prospective buyers needed accommodation and the hotel could provide it.

From the Sale Catalogue:

> 'A motor can be arranged for on application to Mr F Pyke, the Landlord of "The White Lion Hotel".

Also from the Catalogue:

> *Mr W Monk, of Wherwell, Hants, will by appointment show the Estate.*

Will Monk was then an Estate worker and lived on the Old Hill. I have no doubt that Will was in close contact with Fred Pyke over these arrangements.

Colonel Jenkins required two days' notice from intending purchasers wishing to view The Priory.

Builders' Merchants representatives – known as travellers – regularly called on father to solicit orders. I would say that most orders were finalised in the comfort and refreshment of the hotel.

Very few people then owned a car. Most evenings there would be just one in the hotel yard – a Singer Saloon owned by Mr Bernard (Bern) Golding from Cottonworth Farm House.

My father once told me about a break-in at the hotel. A burglar forced open a side frame of the Smoking Room bay window to gain entry into the hotel – the only sash framed window in the building. No doubt father was called in to repair and make good.

I spent many happy hours there with Jack and Victor – though not in the bar, except to pass through it! In my mind I can still hear Mr Pyke calling them from the rear door under the bathroom projection.

Mr Pyke acquired the grassland opposite the hotel garden in the Wherwell Estate Sale.

The story of the cannonball (pictured below the lantern) goes back to the time of the Civil War when Oliver Cromwell was fighting the Stuarts and his men fired some cannonballs at Wherwell Priory. Some fell short of range; one is said to have descended a chimney of the White Lion and another fell at the door. It was later said by Victor that two cannonballs, supposedly from the time, had been in the house, one in the public bar and the other which had previously hung from the lantern before its removal. It appears that an American GI took one home as a souvenir.

The White Lion hotel entrance with landlord Fred Pyke proudly displaying his two conveyances. Note the cannonball suspended below the lantern. *(The late Victor Pyke)*

Looking down Mill Lane – The White Lion prominently displayed on the west wall with Fred Pyke and seated villager. Note the Fullerton Road signpost. (The late Victor Pyke)

The Dressmaker

Wherwell village also had a resident dressmaker in the early part of the twentieth century and before. The service was provided by Sarah Child, my great aunt, from her Ivy Cottage home. Mother, when at school, often stayed at the cottage when great uncle Robert Child was working away from home for long periods. She took a keen and practical interest in the art of dressmaking, as a result that when she left school it became a full-time job for her. Later she was to serve a dressmaking apprenticeship with Parsons and Hart; a well-known departmental store in the High Street, Andover. I remember mother telling me about the shop-walker employed at the store. He wore a black suit with a bowler hat. His duty was to assist customers with their requirements and to direct them to the appropriate department and counter.

A picture of great aunt Sarah Child in a wooden frame with a horse's head either side.

above Attractive oak hall table made over 100 years ago by great uncle Robert Child (seen here in my workshop after restoration).

left Great uncle Robert Child with Vera and myself and his dog 'Lady' at his Ivy Cottage home.

My great uncle's father, Henry Child was a wheelwright, carpenter, postmaster and shopkeeper in 1855.

After leaving school Doris Young, living in Fullerton Road, also worked for my aunt as a dressmaker. Shortly before the Great War, Doris married Harry Taylor, who was then a groom at The Priory. Harry served in the War, as many did from the Estate, and suffered from a gas attack; after the War he became a postman. They lived in one of the cottages on the bank-side in Fullerton Road and later moved to the opposite side.

Wherwell Village Laundry

The laundry service was run by Mrs Holdaway, assisted by Mrs Carter, from her 'May Cottage' home in Fullerton Road. The wash-house and buildings used were mainly sheds at the rear of the cottage. The washing mainly consisted of sheets – heavy in those days. I have memories of seeing them hanging from a number of clothes-lines in the meadow-like area close to the river (now a spacious lawn).

Mrs Holdaway used a donkey and cart for delivery, sometimes with pannier bags strapped to the donkey. After the day's work Fred Young would take the donkey to graze in the rough grass meadow behind his parents' home, further along Fullerton Road. Mr Holdaway was a carpenter and worked for Bill Spratt, whose carpenter's shop and office were just across the road.

Mr and Mrs Holdaway had two children, Jack and Evelyn, who were both at school with me and are in the school photographs. Sadly they both died early in life.

Activities of the Young - the Hornby Railway Club

In 1928 I, together with Victor Pyke and his brother Jack (now sadly both deceased) formed the Wherwell Hornby Railway Club. It proved to be a popular hobby for the railway enthusiasts in the village, of which there were many. Mr Pyke kindly gave us use of the Club Room (now called the Lions Den), and we met every Friday evening from 6.00 pm to 9.00 pm. Mr Pyke also provided us with a fire to keep us warm during the winter evenings.

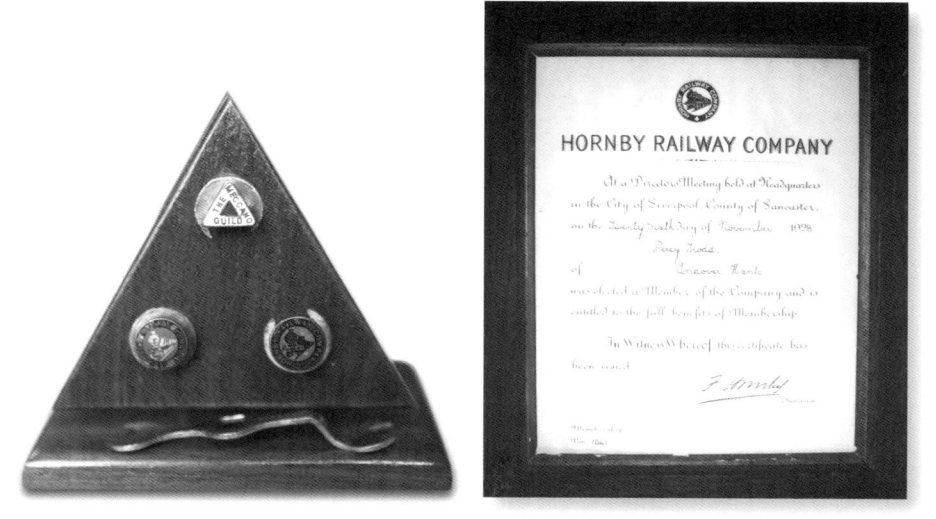

left Display feature showing my Meccano Guild Badge with Hornby Railway Company badges.
right My Membership Certificate of the Hornby Railway Company dated 26 November 1928.

We pooled our stock to form a large double track layout and I constructed various items including stations, signals, a footbridge and fencing. Trestles and tabletops, used on occasions for tea parties, were kept in the room and used to mount the layout. Sometimes it was necessary to use the floor, which was not so clean and comfortable. Once a year visitors (mostly families) would be invited to see the trains in action. We also staged a concert to boost the funds for the purchase of track and accessories. I made a money box for this. The programme would consist of a musical item to open the show, followed by recitations, charades, impersonations, telephone dialogues and a play. We even had a reporter there – the schoolmaster. The shareholders were very pleased with the success of the event. On one occasion we had a trained soloist – an aunt of mine.

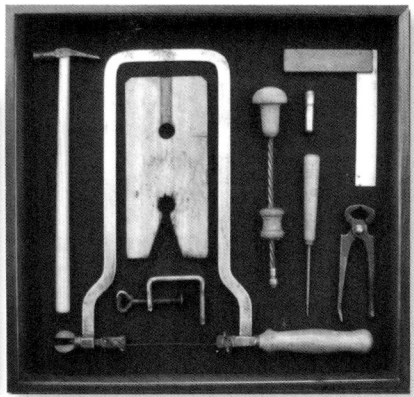

left Restored station footbridge and signal gantry, originally made in 1928 from 3-ply using tools from my Hobbies Fretwork Set. *right* My Hobbies Fretwork set, which I still have.

During school summer holidays an attempt was made to form an outdoor layout at the lower end of Mr Pyke's meadow. I formed a sand and cement track bed for an experimental operation. Sadly it was not successful because the foundations were not up to specification to withstand the heavy weight of the locomotives, and the maintenance costs were proving unacceptable.

In those days it was 'O' gauge and clockwork. One member did have a Bassett-Lawke steam locomotor 4.4.0 – every boy's dream. Sadly it all came to an end when we left school as there were other things to do, but they had been happy days.

Some of the other boys I remember from that time were Jack Trowbridge, Jim Saul, Jim Lewis, Alex Scott, Willy Hand and John Dance.

One year we were privileged to visit Andover Junction Station; as the club's secretary I had obtained the necessary authority. We were met by the station master and given an insight into the day-to-day activities;

Wearing my Parsons & Hart sports coat with my Meccano badge in the early 1930s.

this included the station master's office, engine shed, signal box and ticket office. We were there at the right time to see the Atlantic Coast Express thunder through. Altogether this had proved a very exciting day for those young railway enthusiasts.

As reported in the Andover Advertiser (circa 1929) – "The first annual meeting of the Hornby Railway Co. Ltd was held at the Board Room, White Lion Hotel Club Room, on March 7. Directors' present were Jack Pyke (chairman), J Saul (vice-chairman), Percy Trodd (secretary), together with Jim Lewis, Victor Pyke, A Scott, W Knapp and several shareholders. The chairman gave a glowing account of the progress of the Company, showing possibilities of fine prospects to the shareholders. The Secretary gave his report on the financial position, which was in a most satisfactory condition. Other business of the evening was the arrangements for Easter excursions. The question of adding an Air Service to their railway activities was discussed, some of the board members being enthusiastic aeronauts. Votes of thanks to the officers concluded the proceedings."

Shortly after I left school and working in Andover, I advertised my Hornby collection in the Southern Daily Echo and sold it to a person living in Highfield, Southampton for just £2. I thought I would never use it again and that it would just rust away – an error of judgment on my part.

Croquet

This was my favourite game and was played on my great aunt's lawn at Gavelacre. My mother and grandparents also enjoyed the game. The lawn was so close to the river that in the late summer it was like a wet sponge underfoot. Bowls was also a favourite pastime.

Rear of 'Gavelacre' Wherwell – a family game of bowls which includes my mother.

The Clump

The Clump was a popular beauty spot before the war. It was approached from the pathway in Fullerton Road close to Longbridge; also from the Above Town area which was accessed from 'hairpin bend'. A verse from my poem reads:

> *'Resting awhile at the Clump on a large tree root,*
> *The wind whistling gently through the trees so tall,*
> *Enjoying the scene and the magnificent view with inspiring awe,*
> *Dropping down to the railway and over the line,*
> *"Stop, Look and Listen" read the Notice, there could be a train on the "Nile" to make us smile.'*

(The 'Nile' – name used by the railwaymen.)

My recent climb to the Clump – in bygone days an attractive beauty spot.

Mount Pleasant – the Mount and New Barn Lane

Accessed from New Barn Lane by a steep flight of steps just beyond the railway bridge, the Mount was a popular beauty spot to sit and play; it was also an ideal sun trap. At the top was a bushy yew tree where we could comfortably sit and enjoy the panoramic view down to the village street. It spread out like a huge mushroom and was easy to climb. Smoke rising heavenward from the cottage chimneys gave a scene of peaceful tranquillity, the silence only broken by the ring of the anvil or a passing train.

Sitting on the Mount in the summer sun, my sister and I loved to pick the wild flowers – our favourites were the Little Tom Thumb and the Wiggle-Waggles, together with wild violets and primroses. It was always a colourful scene. When leaving we would often roly-poly down the slope. Sometimes we crossed the railway line for a quick cut back to home. We could hear mother calling us down at meal times.

On the lower part of the Mount we played rounders and other ball games. Here it was on the same level as the railway and afforded a splendid view of the line as it passed through the Mount cutting.

At the time the railway was being constructed in 1884, a pair of thatched cottages stood at the foot of the Mount, they faced the lane and only just a few yards from the railway which at that point was on level ground with the line. Sparks from a passing locomotive (always a factor when climbing the gradient) fell on the thatch and set it alight. Fortunately it was quickly extinguished by the railway construction workers there.

However, there was worse to come, for later when the railway was operational, in a similar incident with sparks from a passing locomotive, the cottages were completely destroyed by fire – there were then no construction workers on hand to put it out.

Vera with her fiancé Bob Gambrill from Andover at the style of Wherwell Mount in 1936.

Walking through the Mount with its tall shady trees hiding the sunshine was a chilly experience. But we loved it; the soft leafy undergrowth was like walking on a magic carpet in perfect silence.

On the high ground to the left of the Mount was a favourite spot for gathering mushrooms. It was early to bed and early to rise for this delicious delight. From the hedgerows we would pick blackberries and sloes, which we would take home to mother. She would make blackberry jam and sloe wine, nothing was wasted.

The Mount was always a popular venue in wintertime for tobogganing and enjoyed by young and old alike. The heaviest snowfall I remember was at Christmastide in 1927 which blocked roads in and out of the village. My contribution was to make a four-seater sledge with metal capped runners, foot rests and cords – used as reins. Although somewhat heavy it was ideal for the fast track run – which was beyond the Mount, and of course there were four of us to haul it back up again to the starting point. Both Victor and Jack Pyke were there with me to enjoy it. I particularly remember a fast run with Victor in the front position for he ended up in the Lane hedge below – not quite a disaster – but we had to pull him out! Victor often reminded me of it. My sister and the older girls also enjoyed the rides. Much to our delight the excitement continued for some days and into the New Year.

The way it was done – snow clearing on Clatford Hill in April 1908.

As it was during Christmas holidays, I wrote about it in a poem which could be sung to the tune of 'Jingle Bells'.

Further up, New Barn Lane, which was overrun with rabbits, passed through a shallow cutting where heavy cart wheels had left deep furrows. On reaching the top it was then a flat open space, and further on to the right a plantation of tall trees, which sloped quite steeply downward to the New Barn area; it was known as Wilkinson's Bank. I remember my first walk there with my brother, when leaving home Norman said to me "we are going to Wilkinson's Bank (a treed area) to get some money"! Of course I believed him. Fronting the plantation was a walnut tree, always an attraction for the boys – and me. The New Barn area consisted of a large barn and just one chalk-walled cottage, which was occupied from time to time - a very quiet and lonely place. Near the barn was a pond.

Taking the path to the right of the cottage would take us up to the copse where we loved to walk. In the springtime it was a carpet of bluebells and primroses – a colourful, magic carpet. Only the occasional crackle of dead wood and the sound of a pheasant flying off as it was disturbed, broke the silence. Another popular pleasure was nut picking.

Snowbound Wherwell in 1952.

Harvest time

But there was yet another pleasure from the Lane - the harvest fields. I loved to watch the horse-drawn binder at work cutting the corn, with stackers following up to stack the corn sheaves. The men always tied their corduroy trousers below the knee with binder twine to protect their legs. Children would bring tea for their fathers in the blue enamelled cans. As the binder moved into the centre, rabbits would be running in all directions – and quite a lot would be caught for the pot. We all ate them in those days, a popular dinner.

Threshing time

Yet another pleasure was to watch the steam traction engine at work with its long wide leather belt attached to the pulley of the threshing machine. There would be at least six or seven men at work; two or three on the rick, possibly three below, and one on the machine. It always puzzled me how they managed to get the traction engine to the site.

A Long Walk

We walked to Andover using New Barn Lane. At New Barn we would turn left and walk across to Andover Road, then to the White House and across the pathway which would bring us to the top of Old Winton Road in about one hour. I suppose living so near to the Lane made it a popular walk for us.

The Fifth of November

For a number of years Guy Fawkes Night was celebrated with a huge bonfire and fireworks on the Mount. Together with my two stalwart pals, Jack and Victor Pyke, and others we were kept busy for some two weeks beforehand scouring the Mount for fallen tree branches, dead wood and twigs, augmented with kindling wood and much more from the carpenter's shop, and a bag of shavings to light it. Sometimes this proved difficult in damp weather but Mr Hand, the blacksmith, was on hand with paraffin soaked rags to light it for us – such a kind family man. Almost all the village children would be there, some with their parents, to enjoy the fun and excitement together, and all with their own fireworks, mostly the hand-held smaller variety with lots of sparklers. Catherine wheels were pinned to a fence post – always a favourite.

Longbridge

During the summer holidays another popular pleasure for the children on hot sunny days was paddling. This took place at the far end of Longbridge by the Common where the water was shallow. Although bare footed we came to no harm.

Many liked to catch minnows using a jam jar tied to a piece of string, and sometimes we would sail a toy boat, usually home-made. Happy chatter and laughter were always part of the scene. The older boys and men could swim in a deep-water area by crossing a meadow from the mill.

It was so exhilarating to be at the mill when the waterwheel was turning and to see the water gushing out into the river from its channel underneath the bridge. When silent, in the still water, I often gazed down on lots of fine trout there – so relaxing. In those bygone days we enjoyed a panoramic view of the river, and gardens, from all along the bridge. I remember mother telling me of the days when she too took corn to the mill for grinding. Apart from generating electricity for The Priory, the end part was also used as a saw mill.

The Raft

The river had a fascination for me – living in the village I was never far from it, and from my bedroom window I could hear the continuous roar of the water as it passed downstream from the weir.

Crossing the water meadows from Wherwell big bridge to Chilbolton – at the half-way style in 1939.

Mona, then my fiancée, at the same half-way style.

Visit to Stonehenge Easter Monday 1938 by my late wife (then my fiancée), her mother and elder sister.

Marjorie Taylor on Longbridge rail in 1931. Marjorie was at school with me and the family lived in Fullerton Road.

One year during the school summer holiday, and with the lure of the river, that together with my school pals Jack and Victor Pyke, plus Willy Knapp, we decided to construct a raft. The lower end of Mr Pyke's meadow, by the river, was the ideal place for it, no one would see us – or so we thought! It was an ambitious project, an opportunity for adventure! We could be pirates, intrepid explorers, or gallant sailors at Trafalgar – the possibilities were endless. Excitement mounted as we mustered large tin drums, timber and planks from the coal yard and father's carpenter's shop, together with scaffold ropes, nails and much more. With perspiration, ingenuity and borrowed tools from father, our vessel was soon built.

We launched the raft onto the water and tied up to an ash tree which cantilevered over the river. After testing for buoyancy and stability, the four adventurers gingerly boarded, each to his corner sporting a navigation pole. It was a delicate balancing act, and then with bated breath we cast off, with the intention of reaching and tying up at Longbridge – 'Longbridge Docks'.

The raft moved to midstream where the water became turbulent and choppy. Our vessel pitched and spun, bobbed up, bobbed down, and despite heroic efforts to steer, followed a course of its own choosing. It was when passing the halfway mark that stout hearts faltered! I was a non-swimmer, so thoughts of pirates, explorers and gallant sailors vanished as discretion became the better part of valour. We poled frantically to reach terra firma on our starboard side. With beating hearts and wet feet, we finally clambered ashore amidst a cluster of willow trees.

Unknown to those fearless four boy sailors as they plied their course, the dreaded Colonel (Colonel A E Jenkins) had spotted the boys on the river, when out riding his white horse – he would of course! The Colonel was furious with anger and dashed to The White Lion to vent his wrath – the boys will be put on a charge for this in his rapid discourse. For those intrepid adventurers it was a sharp reminder to stay on dry land! Here are two lines from a poem I wrote about the incident:
No, never again did they sail the Test,
Their plans were scuppered and laid to rest.

A Lucky Escape

I only remember one boy falling into the river – the younger son of Mr and Mrs Archie Parker who then lived at Winchester Corner Cottages. Adrian was just four years old when he fell in from the riverbank steps opposite the cottage, used for dipping water, and was quickly carried under the bridge in the fast flowing turbulent water to some distance downstream. Fortunately a cyclist approaching the bridge from Chilbolton spotted Adrian, dashed to the riverbank, pulled him out and carried him home to his mother – shaken but unharmed. Adrian told me later than he had to stay in bed the next day.

Archie Parker was a carpenter and worked for father at times, his wife was caretaker at the new school. After the disastrous fire at The Priory in 1944 he did much of the restoration work which included building a new roof.

above Mr and Mrs Archie (Curly) Parker at their Winchester Corner home, Wherwell in the 1920s.

right The Wherwell Cockatrice made by Archie Parker.

Painting of a Wherwell village scene by Archie Parker.

The Village Blacksmith

Mr Frederick Hand was the village blacksmith in the twenties and early thirties. He lived with his wife and family in Forge Cottage. We were good friends and neighbours as his garden extended to our cottage boundary.

An early photograph (circa 1905) of the blacksmith's shop with Richard Vearncombe - opposite is Forge Cottage.

To lighten the north bedroom of Forge Cottage a new window, made in the carpenter's shop, was added – the cost was £4. (All the front facing windows were small, as it was with most cottages.)

Mr and Mrs Hand in 1933. They gave the Trodd family the original prior to leaving Wherwell.

The blacksmith shop with the Mount beyond.

His skill was very much in evidence in specialist work other than shoeing. An iron gate, fashioned and made by him, stands at the main west entrance to The Priory, by the Andover Lodge. Wrought ironwork was a speciality and included fireplaces for logs and fire dogs, door handles and latches, weather vanes, lamp standards and even metal flowers. He was a true craftsman.

The other blacksmith working with him was Thomas Baverstock, affectionately known to us as Tommy Stock. He lived at Chilbolton in the appropriately named 'Horseshoe Cottage' and always wore a peaked cap. There was also an apprentice from Leckford, named Sillence. In earlier days mother could remember four men working at the forge. The blacksmiths started work early; in the summertime it was six o'clock with breakfast at eight. Saturday was early closing at noon.

There was always plenty of repair work and sharpening to be done. Harrows would be left by farmers for sharpening of the tines (spikes) or the making and fitting of new ones. There were two forges and two large anvils, most of the time they were both in use. We could clearly hear the ringing sound of the anvils from our cottage. It was delightful, especially in the summertime with the windows open. There were very few cars on the road; it was mostly horse and carts, steam wagons and steam engines.

Pony-drawn cart made by father (after retirement) for Kurt, the blacksmith. Sadly it came to grief near his Appleshaw home.

Wheel Bonding (or Binding)

In addition to father's building work, his skill as a wheelwright was appreciated by the local farmers and hauliers as he kept their cartwheels turning.

In addition to the wheels, new shafts were made and fitted to carts and wagons. These would be hand-sawn from a length of four-inch thick timber – always kept for this purpose (ash), prepared, shaped and finished to pattern then treated.

This work was vital in those days as carts and wagons were used extensively for transport on farms and roads. Repairing the heavy wooden wheels entailed making and fitting new spokes and felloes *(curved outer sections of a wheel)*. Each felloe was joined by a dowel and left with a gap, which would be tightly closed and left solid after binding. Sometimes a new hub had to be made. The wheel was then treated with red-oxide and rolled up to the blacksmith's shop for bonding.

The Bonding Process

Wheel binding was a skilled operation. The blacksmith would first measure the circumference of the wheel to assess the length of iron required, allowing for shrinkage. A special hearth had to be assembled in the forge to form a tunnel of fire to make the new iron hoop or tire that bound the felloes. When the new iron tire was ready for bonding the wheel would be taken to the circular iron platform, which was in the blacksmith's yard. The platform had an opening in the centre to recess the hub, which was firmly screwed down to secure the wheel. Using heavy lifting tongs the red-hot tire was carried across the road to the bonding platform and placed on the wheel, then driven on with sledge hammers and quickly doused with water. The contraction made the bonding complete.

Before the operation buckets of water had to be pumped from the cottage well; drums, cans and tubs were filled and placed around the platform. It was a case of all hands to the pump!

Wheel bonding was done on a Saturday morning, unlike today it was always a quieter time. It was an interesting and absorbing process which I always enjoyed watching. Sometimes flames would shoot up from the felloes but were quickly doused.

Shoeing

Making horseshoes was commonplace in those days for shoeing was an important part of the business. There were many working cart horses, not only from Wherwell, but also Chilbolton and Fullerton. There were also many hunters at Wherwell Estate (the stables were in Mill Road

– the back way to The Priory). Quite often two horses needed to be shod at the same time.

It was fascinating to watch, and again I loved to stand and gaze at the whole operation. Wearing a leather apron slit down the middle, the blacksmith held the hoof between his knees and, withdrawing the nails with a wrench, he removed the old shoe. After filing down with a rasp the new hot shoe was placed on the hoof using a tong and nailed on (that was the part which worried me). There was always an unpleasant burning smell with smoky fumes rising from the hoof. The nails penetrated the side of the hoof and were twisted off, again with a wrench. A rasp was used to finish the job.

Holding the heavy hoof between the knees was a difficult, strenuous and back-aching job for the blacksmith. Mr Hand was forced to resign in 1933 as shoeing had caused a back problem and he decided to leave the village. His loyal servant Tommy also left the forge.

Father was devastated and concerned for Mr Hand – he was a good friend and neighbour. Furthermore, the village was losing a skilled blacksmith. When the anvils had fallen silent, it was the end of an era and sadly things were never quite the same again.

But it was not only the forge that was lost. One room in Forge Cottage was used as a cycle shop, here the cyclist (of which there were many) could buy a new wheel, tyre or tube, a new puncture repair outfit, a can of oil or a tin of carbide for the then popular acetylene lamp and much more. A new Hercules bicycle for mother cost £2.19.6d (unusual about it was a back-pedal brake). This now ended.

Mr Hand had been a stalwart of the Methodist chapel. In those days the only occasion he used his car on a Sunday was to collect a circuit preacher. He was a kind-hearted family man, always considerate and helpful. I often saw him with a daisy between his lips. I think it was his favourite little flower because his younger daughter was named Daisy.

In the still air early on Christmas mornings he and his son Fred, both being brass instrumentalists, would stand on the bonding platform and play a selection of carols to the delight of all.

The Cordwainer

Living close to the blacksmith was James Tovey. The Tovey family were prominent members of the Wherwell village community around the turn of the twentieth century, and before. James was a cordwainer *(shoemaker)*, as was his father before him. The end room of the cottage (near the Lodge) was his cobbler's workshop, with access to a small timber built shop extension, entranced from the pathway to the rear of the cottage. Hanging inside the shop door was an original house-type spring held bell which would ring when the door opened.

The shop was stocked with footwear of all kinds, including the hobnail boots commonly worn by the workmen in those days. He was kept busy not only with orders from The Priory, the heavy workload of repairs for its many staff and farm workers, but also making new footwear to order. Normally he closed his shop at 7.00 pm. The smell of new leather was especially nice. During the summer months plimsolls and sandals would hang outside the shop to attract customers.

The much respected Wherwell Tovey family in 1908.

Wherwell High Street, beyond the Priory Lodge can be seen Mr Tovey's cordwainer's shop.

James Tovey was my great uncle, his two brothers were also cordwainers - William with a shop at Longparish and Edgar with a shop in High Street, Salisbury. When James died in 1928 the cottage was occupied by Fred Taylor and his family. I remember their twin girls, Freda and Rosa, also Pearl. He used the shop as a grocery business and kept a Ford van for his rounds. After his passing the shop was demolished by father and the opening to the end room filled in.

Will Monk was also a Wherwell cobbler. He lived in the end cottage on the Old Hill and worked his craft in just a small galvanised ironclad wooden shed at the end of his garden pathway. It was probably less than six feet square with a small window and narrow doorway. After James Tovey's passing, Will did our footwear repairs and it was usual for me to take the repairs to him. I have memories of him sitting up close to the window carrying out his work, however being small it was always in a muddle. Will Monk married Elsie Carter who lived next to the Taylor family on the bankside in Fullerton Road. Elsie was the organist at the Primitive Methodist Chapel.

Boot and Shoe Merchant - the Tovey family name displayed over their High Street shop in Salisbury 1906.
(reproduced by permission of the Francis Frith Collection)

But the family tradition of cordwainers continued. Trained by a great uncle James Tovey, my uncle, Frederick Blackall, owned a footwear shop in the High Street at Shaftesbury. The shop window displayed a full range of footwear which included the popular 'K' Shoes. All repairs were done on the premises – as it was at Wherwell.

Further along Shaftesbury's High Street was a Drapers and Outfitters, a large double fronted shop. This business was owned and run by my uncle, William Salisbury, with his name in gold lettering above the shop. There were several assistants in the drapery department, whilst in the outfitting it was Norman (my brother) who was in sole charge.

Much of the clothing stock was then sold in shillings and pence. In the drapery department quite often the price would end with farthings – such as 19/11¾d. For change the customer would receive a packet of pins (commonly used in the home for many things). Then too it could be priced in guineas (21 shillings). Clothing alterations for customers were done on the premises. I was allowed in the drapery section to talk to the assistants but not to stay. In the outfitting I could chat with Norman, but only if there were no customers to be served. (My Christmas present was usually a pair of socks and a tie.)

I recall some happy holidays there, my bedroom overlooked the lawn at the rear of the shop. Compared with our Wherwell cottage, every room was so much larger with lots of space everywhere. My aunt did the cooking and much of the housekeeping, but she did have a live-in helper.

Uncle owned a motor car, it was a bull-nosed Morris Cowley Tourer and my aunt was the driver – unusual in those days for it was a man's prerogative for many years. From time to time he visited his parents living in Coat, Somerset and I was with them to enjoy the ride on two occasions. I think it must have been summertime as the hood was always folded down at the back. Sitting in the back I found it rather draughty but a car ride in those days was so exciting, it was an adventure and not many children had the privilege.

Later the Cowley was replaced with a new Morris Oxford. A much improved model with a flat fronted radiator – but still a tourer. Norman now did most of the driving, something he enjoyed doing – especially with a new car. There were journeys to Wherwell for aunt and uncle to visit her parents (my grandparents). This was always on a Sunday when the shop would be closed. Awaiting them would be a delicious cream tea with fresh Guernsey butter and milk from The Priory and newly baked bread and dough cakes from the bakehouse – probably much more, including soft fruit from the garden. Vera and I were often invited to tea.

Shaftesbury was such a delightful place to live and work. Memories for me of the lovely walks which I enjoyed, almost as if on a mountain top, with magnificent views across the valleys below and far beyond, with many seats along the way to rest awhile and gaze. It was idyllic and so bracing. The town had its own gas works and could be seen far below in the valley on the west side. No doubt the town also generated its own electricity. Then too the famous Gold Hill, which I walked up and down with Norman.

It was soon after my grandparents retired from their shop in Wherwell that my Uncle, Irving Blackall, who had been working in the bakehouse, decided with his wife and daughter, to also move to Shaftesbury. There he set up his own grocery and provisions shop in the town. No doubt with a little help and encouragement from his brother and sister.

Norman on banjo with the Arcadians.

While in Shaftesbury, probably in the early 'thirties, Norman bought a banjo and with the help of a correspondence course he perfected his playing. He then formed a five-piece dance band which he named the Arcadians. He also played the clarinet and ukulele. All the players wore dress suits. The clarinet was originally owned by my great uncle, James Tovey, an earlier village musician. I still have it.

For my journeys to Shaftesbury mother would take me to Andover and put me on a Royal Blue coach. On arrival at Shaftesbury my aunt would be there to meet me.

However, my first car ride was with Jack and Victor Pyke in their uncle's open top Buick car to Winchester, for a performance of the famous Bertram Mills Circus. What I still vividly remember – a man encased in leather, being shot out of a cannon and landing in a huge net – what excitement!

above my favourite Red Funnel paddle steamer 'Gracie Fields' –sunk during the evacuation from Dunkirk. *(courtesy of Ken Braxton)*

top left A day out on the Royal Pier, Southampton in 1936 – from where I enjoyed popular paddle steamer trips to the Isle of Wight *(taken by Vera)* .

left Vera in the 1930s.

Chapter 5

Education

The Old School

The Church of England Wherwell Village Old School was situated on a strip of land to the left of the old hill and just a few yards beyond the arched railway bridge. To the left of the approach was the school garden plots which extended down to the railway fence. To the right, separated by huge elm trees, was the boys' playground.

A public footpath (still used) passed through it, close to the rear of Hillside Cottages, the school frontage and the girls' playground, and continued further to exit near the hairpin bend. There was a public seat, made of iron, in a clearing near the exit which overlooked the road and village (a favourite resting place for me before going on to Above Town and The Clump beyond).

The school was built of brick and flint with a pitched roof and a plastered ceiling. The building was approximately 36 feet long and 16 feet wide. Two small cloakrooms, each about seven feet square, were added at each end of the frontage with facing entrance doors. An inside door provided access to the classrooms. The main windows were at the front of the school, either side of the fireplace in the larger room. In addition there were high narrow windows at the rear.

To the left of the building was the infants' classroom, which was square in shape with a fixed partition and connecting door to the larger senior classroom. (I remember the door well with its strings of coloured beads which covered the glass panel.) The open fireplace was in the south facing wall. The class faced the partition, with teacher's table and blackboard. There was a clock over the cloakroom doorway, but in my early days I was unable to read the time.

In the much larger classroom (seniors), the desks were arranged longitudinally for the children to face the open fireplace. Miss Tyrer was the headteacher and I think this was done for her benefit because she did feel the cold. Often I remember her holding a double sheet of newspaper to the fire to draw it up. It was quite effective but sometimes would burst into flames and quickly pushed up the chimney. There was a fireplace at the north end of the classroom, but not normally used. With heavy cast-iron end supports, the long sloping top desks accommodated four. Backless, bench type wooden forms provided the seating. Inkwells were recessed to avoid spillage.

Pupils at the old school each wearing a Victorian style postman's helmet and holding a letter (circa 1919) – Norman is seated left.

Miss Tyrer lived with my great aunt, Julie Green, at Gavelacre Cottage, next to Fred Young's dairy. They were both members of the Wherwell Choral Society and both are pictured with the choir in their Banner winning success (see Chapter 9 – Religious and Other Groups).

Doris Hayes, the school pianist, lived with her mother and two brothers, Alan and Percy, and all attended the village school. The family lived at no. 3 Freelands Cottages in Fullerton Road. Alan was my class-mate when we moved to the new school. Sadly, Percy was killed in a motorcycle accident during the War.

Because of my left-handedness, writing was difficult for me when I started school. Miss Horne, my teacher, insisted I hold the pencil with my right hand. I sat near to the front of class where she could keep an eye on me, but when she turned away the pencil was back in my left hand. Miss Horne was persistent with me – it had to be my right hand and at times she stood over me. I did overcome it – I had to!

Pupils at the old school (circa 1920). *Second row 9th from left* – myself. *Third row 4th from left* – Norman. *Standing centre right* – Miss E Horne (my teacher).

During my years at the old school, I still remember my three seating positions – one in the infants and two in the seniors. For me they were happy years.

Returning home from school twice daily, a pleasant walk, particularly in dry weather, was across the Fairpiece and the field beyond, enjoying the song of the skylark as it soared above me, picking blackberries when ripe, then down the lane, under the railway bridge and home.

Living in Hillside Cottages in those days were at no. 1 Mr and Mrs Howard with their son George and daughter Edith. Both were at school with me and are pictured in the school photographs. Mr Howard was of a stately bearing and the Priory butler.

Mrs Smith lived at no. 2 with her daughters, Muriel and Doris. Both were at the school in earlier days with Norman, and later, when 12, all

Pupils at the old school (circa 1922) – *front row 4th from left* Vera; *second row 2nd from left* myself; *back row 4th from left* Norman. (The last school photograph of Norman before he attended Andover Grammar School).

Pupils at the old school in 1927
Left to right – back row Geoffrey Holloway, Percy Trodd, Alan Hayes, Bill Rowles, Fred Hand, Tom Holloway, George Howard
Third row Lily Purver, Edith Howard, Louise Collins, Evelyn Holdaway, Kathleen Boucher, Dorothy Beachamp, Dorothy Boucher and Marjorie Taylor
Second row Walter Skeates, Mabel Holloway, Doris Hayes, Vivien Flemington, Ernest Nutley, Harold Hams, Jack Holdaway, Jim Lewis, Jack Pyke, Jim Saul.
Front row Marjorie Butler, Marjorie Stagg, Edwina Rodden, Margaret Roughton, Lilian Hams, Marjorie Hams, Vera Trodd, Christine Prangley

attended the Andover Grammar School. Sadly Mr Smith was killed in the Battle of the Somme, during the Great War. Before he was called up, he too worked for the Priory Estate.

Mr Rhys followed Miss Tyrer as headteacher, his accommodation was with Mr and Mrs Tom Spratt at Southcroft, Fullerton Road. Changes were made, firstly the desks were turned for the class to face the partition (as in the infants' room). There would be no more window gazing – more attention to the blackboard. In addition there was now the threat of the cane, which Mr Rhys kept on his table in front of class – and me - but more often in his hand! The shame of standing in front of class for a stroke – or more - of the cane was not only humiliating but it also hurt. It happened to me once – for climbing a tree. Discipline and good behaviour were strict, there was no talking during lessons.

The exterior frontage area, used for assembly and drill, was formed of concrete and extended to the whole length of the school building and outwards to the public footpath. The school bell was rung for assembly.

The lavatories were back-to-back at the rear of the school building and approached separately from the playgrounds and pathways. There was no doorway at the entrance to the boys' urinal – it was an open space, probably because it was small with single access and perhaps for ventilation, for it was always smelly.

There was no water supply and no lighting at the school. During wintertime the school closed at 3.30 pm; to redress this the dinner-time was reduced by half-an-hour. Mrs Smith lived in the thatched cottage on the Old Hill, opposite the school entrance. In the heat of summer she would draw up a bucket of water from her deep well and place it on the concrete plinth together with enamel mugs for the thirsty children to dip in and help themselves. This kind gesture was appreciated by the children – and myself, but especially those who were unable to go home at dinner-time.

A model aeroplane, which I made from cardboard, hung from the ceiling.

An unusual lesson – one hot summer's day I remember sitting with my class underneath the tall beech trees across the top ridge of the Fairpiece for a drawing lesson. The landscape was perfect for this, it was a happy day for me and my class with good results. Sadly I have no recollection of a repeat of this but it is mentioned in my poem 'Memories of a Favourite Walk'.

From time to time during summer months we played cricket on the Fairpiece. I was not a star player but it was exciting. The downside was the sloping ridges for the ball frequently ended up deep down on the railway line – fortunately volunteers quickly retrieved it.

The school nurse would attend from time to time to check our hair. This was done in the girls' cloakroom. There were other callers, including the attendance officer to check the register. Each day the register was ticked, the teacher would call our name and each would respond by saying 'present'.

When leaving school one day, the Old Hill railway bridge near the old school tempted a Fullerton boy from my class to walk across the top face of a side wall in the downward direction. I watched him but it was a risky thing to do.

Coming from a musical family, I enjoyed the weekly singing lesson under Miss Tyrer, with Doris Hayes, our excellent pianist. There was a special song for each month of the year, two of which I remember:

> (i) Come out, 'tis now September,
> The hunter's moon begun …

> (ii) O who will o'er the Downs so free,
> O who will with me ride …
> (June/July)

On Ash Wednesday we all walked in file to the church for a Lenten service. One of the hymns I remember was 'Forty days and forty nights'. After the service we were allowed home.

On Empire Day, 24 May, the maypole (always kept in the infants' classroom alongside the west wall) was erected on the girls' playground for a session of maypole dancing, each with a coloured ribbon which plaited around the pole in a downward direction.

Old school photograph circa 1928
Left to right – back row Bill Rowles, Ernest Nutley, Jim Lewis, Jack Holdaway and Alan Hayes
Third row   Hazel Dowdell, Louise Collins, Dorothy Beachamp, Kathleen Boucher, Marjorie Taylor, Edith Howard and
                  Doris Hayes
Second row Marjorie Stagg, Margaret Roughton, Lilian Hams, Mabel Holloway and Vera Trodd
Front row   Tom Holloway, Geoffrey Holloway, Walter Blades, Jack Pyke, Percy Trodd, Jim Saul and Jack Purver

Just recently, when looking through the Andover Advertiser, I caught sight of the following. "Wherwell – Friday, 5 October 1877. Following an examination at the school the report of HM Inspector was that the children had done creditably well. There were no failures in reading or writing but four in arithmetic." This was achieved without calculators and computers, which speaks well for the blackboard – and with only two teachers.

School Prizes

My three school prize books, still part of my treasured possessions, suitably inscribed in beautiful handwriting:

Still William   *Presented to Percy Trodd (in each)*
                            for good work 1927-28

Martin Rattler   For a neat garden plot –
spring 1928

The Mysteries of Saddleworth   For general proficiency –
for Christmas Term
With best wishes
Mr and Mrs A H Olliff
(Board of Governors)

For my garden plot work I used Mr Pyke's tools, which I would collect on my way to school. I still have one of my school reports

My prized possessions – Day School and Sunday School prize books.

The New School

Built by Chivers and Sons of Devizes in Longparish Road, it was an excellent site. Compared to the old school it was a palace, easily accessible and on level ground with a superb playground. It opened in 1929 with a new headmaster, Mr Phillip Leigh. Miss Burns was in charge of the infants' class. I was one of the first pupils to attend.

The school had two classrooms, the same as its predecessor. These were more spacious, bright and airy with a folding partition dividing the two and of equal size. The windows, each side, were large and spaced to give adequate light and fitted with angled draught excluder glazed frames of about 10" in height. With no ceiling, the roof space was left open, additional light was provided by the matching size dormer windows which extended into the roof space. The headmaster's room was at the south end, entranced from a passageway.

The cloakrooms were more than twice the size of those at the old school, now with windows and the luxury of a set of five wash-basins piped with cold water supply only (which most children had never seen). Water was hand pumped from a well, the pump room was in the north-west corner of the building, connected by a passageway which extended from the boys' cloakroom. (I did try my hand at the pump.) As with the old school there was no lighting – not even a candle! The lavatories were either side of the assembly ground, away from the school. Although somewhat similar to the old school they were much larger and improved.

A feature of the school was the substantial verandah which connected with the two cloakrooms and provided excellent cover for the classroom entrance doors. It was supported by elegantly styled pillars.

Unlike the old school where we sat on forms (no backs) with long sloping heavy desks, we now had hinged top two-seater desks with a convenient storage compartment and comfortable chairs. We faced the blackboard, which was much larger and fixed to the wall. It was the focal point of learning and Mr Leigh made good use of it with his teaching for it captivated me, not only with mathematics but with drawings, always so quick and so beautifully done. Mr Leigh was so adept and so masterly. Of course, it was for us to copy. During lessons you could hear a pin drop, we had to be attentive. Discipline remained very strict.

There was a useful building in the school ground beyond the assembly area, it was intended to be used for cookery lessons, but with lack of equipment it made little progress during my time. It was used by children at lunch-time – a place to eat their sandwiches, which for many was bread and jam or cheese, with margarine as butter, as it was at the old school. Not many were as fortunate as me to walk home in just a few minutes.

Senior pupils and Headmaster at the new school (circa 1929)
Left to right – back row Marjorie Stagg, Marjorie Hams, Edith Howard, Marjorie Taylor, Evelyn Holdaway, Doris Hayes
Third row   Christine Prangley, Daphne Howard, Marjorie Chadwick, Schoolmaster Philip Leigh, Ellen Eccles, Vera Trodd, Frances Merryfield, Lilian Hams, Mabel Holloway and Freda Nutley
Second row Enid Trowbridge, Edie Coleman, Frances Hammond, Winnie Roughton, Edwina (Teddy) Rodden and Hazel Dowdell
Front row   Percy Trodd, Jack Trowbridge, Willie Knapp, Jack Holdaway, Jack Taylor, Fred Taylor, George Stagg, George Tarrant, Tom Holloway, George Howard, Tom Merryfield, Alan Hayes and Jim Lewis

Father tendered for the school construction but the much larger firm of Chivers Building Contractors offered the lowest tender, though not by much. Three years later father was awarded the contract to repaint the school. I assisted him with this work – I was now driving his Ford lorry. All the paint for this was specified by Hampshire County Council.

School Monitor

Soon after the school opened Mr Leigh called me to his room. He had decided to appoint a school monitor and that I had been chosen. I expressed my willingness to serve the school and that it was an honour to be selected. He went on to detail my duties and provided me with his school whistle – there was no school bell.

For me, this was a responsibility. I would have some authority, a sense of purpose and trust. Fortunately, I lived near the school as good timekeeping was essential. Any bad behaviour or disobedience had to be reported.

From the verandah I would blow the whistle at 9.00 am to bring the pupils to the parade ground and line up, then another whistle to file in an orderly single line into school. This was repeated after playtime at 11.00 am, after lunch at 1.30 pm and after playtime at 3.00 pm. There were other occasions to use the whistle, such as sports and physical exercises.

Pupils at the new school (circa 1930)
Back row Percy Trodd, George Howard, Jim Lewis, Jack Holdaway and Alan Hayes
Front row Victor Pyke, Jack Taylor, Jack Trowbridge, Fred Taylor and Willie Knapp

School Days

Mr Leigh lived in one of the bungalows at South Harewood and used his 4-seater tourer car (the norm in those days) for transport to and from school. One day he arrived at school with a puncture. I was there and said to him "I can change the wheel for you, Sir". This I did. I had done it with father's car, which was similar.

On one occasion when our pianist Doris Hayes was away, I was proud to be asked to play for the morning assembly.

For the first time we had examinations at the end of term – something we had not experienced before, and a school report to take home to our parents. It was signed by Mr Leigh. I still have one – with my treasures.

A delightful view looking north from Winchester Corner with Greenwick Cottages and school in the background.

Chapter 6

The Carpenter's Shop

Father started his carpentry and building business in 1919. A new carpenter's shop was erected and extended over the years to provide storage for timber and building materials. The original carpenter's shop was made into a garage.

There were three benches in use. The joinery work consisted of windows, doors and frames, staircases and much more. These were used for alterations, extensions and replacements. Repair work was also a speciality. Joinery for new buildings was supplied by a joinery manufacturer. Other work included making ladders, hand-steps, trestles, wheelbarrows and even garden furniture.

Collection of father's old hand tools used in the carpenter's shop at Wherwell, many now more than 100 years old.

More old tools in father's collection.

Normally there would be one or two carpenters working in the shop each day with an apprentice, also a painter. At least seven men living in the village worked for father at different times. There were also three from Chilbolton and Leckford. Some were long-term and included two apprentices – Jack Hayes, then living at Room Cottages, and Bob Millard from Broxton Court Cottages. All the carpenters wore white aprons, as did the painters. The carpenter's shop, the blacksmith's shop and the cordwainer's shop were very much an active part of the village scene. There were very few power tools before the War. Mains electricity arrived in 1934 and was provided by the Wessex Electricity Supply Company; initially the power lines ended at our cottage.

On my way home from school I always paused at the blacksmith's shop - it fascinated me, especially when work was in progress at the anvil. Then it was on to the carpenter's shop, something quite different, where I could talk to the men and use my inquisitive mind. I loved the smell of new wood, especially when it was freshly cut or planed. In my youth I became quite adept with the tools and often assisted father.

As children we did not have climbing frames, swings and rides as they have today, but we did have trees to climb. I used father's scaffold ropes for swings from tree branches and carpenter's stools and scaffold planks for see-saws.

Expansion and Building Construction Work

Father's business rapidly gained momentum and required an office; this was built in the yard. An important further acquisition was a piece of land known as Hall Meadow in Chilbolton. This was partly located behind the old village hall. A concrete bridge had to be built to gain access to it from the road. A large shed and workshop were erected to assist with work in the village. It was an ideal builder's yard. Underneath the topsoil was an unlimited quantity of clean white gravel which was used for concrete work. A new Model 'T' one-ton Ford lorry was purchased for transport. It was also used, with canvas covered tilt, on Saturday afternoons for conveyance of the Wherwell Cricket Club team to their matches in the area. Portable bench type seating was provided either side with a step ladder for entrance at the rear.

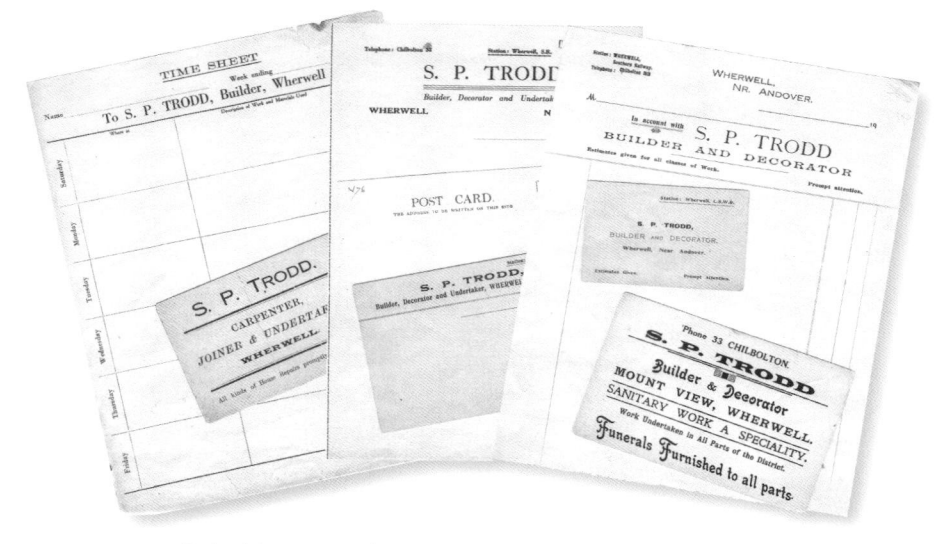

Father's business cards, stationery items and workman's time sheet.

Within a short space of time father was working at all the large properties in Wherwell, Chilbolton, Leckford and Fullerton; also at Manor House, Newton Stacey for Colonel Lloyd and thereafter for Mr Govett. There was extensive work for Wherwell Priory and Estate, which included Manor Farm and Dublin Farm. At the latter a large granary was built on staddle stones near the site of the old chalk-pit chapel. The Police House at Clatford was also built by father; the materials for which were specified by Hampshire County Council, including the cement. There was also some rebuilding of Longbridge in the main-stream area.

Mounted on staddle stones, the granary construction by father at Dublin Farm, Wherwell (pictured here in 2002).

A major repair to the Priory Estate water keepers' punt was carried out in our yard, which entailed a complete rebuild with new flat bottom. I liked to watch the progress being made when home from school. When restoration was complete I was there to see father pouring in hot pitch to seal the bottom and make it water-tight. This treatment was extended to the lower part of both sides. The punt was used for weed cutting and often seen on the river from our cottage. It always seemed to me to be somewhat leisurely work, but of course that was not so, probably more of a balancing act with both water keepers in the punt. The water keepers then were Mr Combridge (Head) living in the main Andover Road Lodge and Mr Scott living in the Winchester Road Lodge.

The Priory Estate employed two carpenters mainly for maintenance work. Mr Greenwood was in charge of this, he lived in the first Priory Cottage opposite the White Lion frontage. Next to him lived the Harding family. Mr Harding was Head Gardener at the Priory. His son Dennis and wife Phyllis are very much a respected and well-known part of the village community.

Weed cutting on the river Test at Freelands, Wherwell
(it could be that the waterkeeper in the punt is Tom Smith).

The riverbank, upstream on the east side of big bridge, Winchester Road, was piled for some distance where there was access to the river for the fishermen. Often I would see them there – a favourite fishing spot. I used some of the surplus oak for making furniture.

There was even work at the White Lion - not for the landlord but, with his approval, at the request and expense of a long-stay fisherman a larger window was made in the carpenter's shop to replace the smaller one in the room which he regularly occupied – he complained of insufficient light.

My cousin, Cyril Baxter, served an apprenticeship as a hairdresser. In the late twenties he used to spend his summer holiday staying with my grandparents in Fullerton Road. I remember Cyril telling me how he regularly visited the White Lion Hotel to cut the fishermen's hair in their rooms. Probably it was just for pocket money – with a trout thrown in! He later owned his own hairdressing business in Hartley Wintney where he lived.

During school holidays I was always keen to go with father to his building sites and properties where he and his men were working, particularly in Chilbolton – an opportunity for me to ride in our new lorry but always

In later years, examples of my furniture and cabinet productions much of which was made in father's carpenter shop. The clocks and tambourine displayed are from my great aunt Sarah Child.

asking first "where are you going – can I come dad?" On more than one occasion and in the presence of father, it was said to me by the owner 'your father is an artist, and you are like your father'. What a nice compliment.

I was at the granary construction at Dublin Farm when the floor was being laid, using the floor cramps and trying my hand at driving in nails. Father was watching and said to me "Don't leave too many pennies on the floor!" I was puzzled because I had no pennies in my pocket, but of course what he meant was that when I missed the nail the hammer would leave an impression the size of an old penny. His men working there would say to me "Put the hammer in your right hand". But then there were more pennies than nails because of my left-handedness!

In the early twenties a London architect, Ernest R Barrow, lived at Chilbolton Cottage. Having seen father building the new part of our cottage at Wherwell he asked if he would do some work for him. As a result the impressive porch extension with a room above and oriel window was built in the centre area of the cottage in 1923. This was a landmark for father and much admired.

Extension to Chilbolton Cottage as constructed by father in 1923.

In later years Mrs Cameron acquired Chilbolton Cottage. She was so impressed with the porch construction that father was asked to carry out work for her. As a result, in 1931 a new building was erected at the south end of the property for servants' accommodation. It was built in line with, and beyond, the existing small cottage at the roadside. A wider access area was provided from the roadside with a spacious new brick built garage fitted with sliding doors and windows. In addition a new 9" brick and flint wall was built along the boundary line of the property, stepped up with the rising ground to the high point of the garden. When completed it presented a pleasing feature of the village scene. In addition to the new buildings, repair work and alterations were required to the main cottage area, also to the small cottage. I myself was working there with father, mostly with repair work.

All the concrete was mixed by hand, the ballast being turned twice dry and twice wet and wheeled to the trenches – usually done by two workmen. The gravel was drawn from our yard by horse and cart, hired from Fred Young with Busty in charge, he was strong, energetic and had worked for Fred Young probably since he left school. The scaffolding in those days consisted of wooden poles tied together with hemp ropes, each staging consisted of four planks, with no safety rails.

When the pitched roof was being built on to the servants' quarters Mrs Cameron was furious with father saying it was too high, it had to be lowered. The building was at right angles to the main cottage and blighted her view – something she had not considered when the plans were drawn up. She was a strong-minded and determined person. Her son, Freddie, owned a private aeroplane. Of a somewhat frivolous character he would fly over the cottage and wave to his mother; sadly he was later killed in a flying accident.

To the south of Chilbolton Cottage (boundaried by the new brick and flint wall) lived Harry Stanley. The south room at the end of his cottage (part of a pair) was used as a sweet shop, entranced from the roadside and open seven days a week – as did Hunt's shop. Behind the counter the wall was lined with shelves and stocked full with bottled sweets – as was the window. A similar spring held house-type door bell (as used by the cordwainer at Wherwell) was audible enough to alert Harry when in his garden. A black couch was provided in the shop for customers to sit and wait. Norman and I often called in to patronise and chat with him. I remember him for his large bushy moustache. I remember too the red brick floor which in heavy downpours of rain was often under water, as was the roadway, as it flowed down the track alongside the shop from the gateway to the high rising ground behind, which extended to Eastman's Farm and used for grazing and hay. When Jack Eastman was hay-making the local children would be there to watch and enjoy. Harry Stanley was also a part-time waterkeeper.

Still seen in Wherwell and Chilbolton – manhole covers with father's name.

Room Cottages were offered to my father *en bloc* for £1,000. Money was not easy to come by then and reluctantly he had to decline. With low rents, probably only about 5s 0d then or less, he thought maintenance costs would outstrip the income. Looking back, it was a missed opportunity, but that is how life was.

Mrs Smith and her son Edward (known as Ted) lived in the picturesque thatched cottage which bordered the roadside and Room Cottages. When Ted left school he was a shepherd boy looking after Farmer Rose's sheep.

He remained single and in later years worked for Kennedy and Kemp Limited at Harewood Forest Works, Longparish. His method of transport was a Royal Enfield motorcycle – until I sold him a car! After his mother passed away Ted sold the cottage. A bungalow was built for his living in a retained area of the garden, independently accessed from the roadside. Ted's brother Frank lived in Room Cottages.

Mr W Baylis was then living at Chilbolton Manor. Father also did work for him as he did in later years for Mr G Painter. Mr Baylis always rode his bicycle to Wherwell to see father. All accounts for work done there were submitted to the Ecclesiastical Commissioners, Winchester.

Mr and Mrs Wallis lived at Church Farm House, their farmyard bordered up to our meadow, with lots of chicken and a fine orchard. Father also undertook building repairs for them.

In the early twenties plots of land in Upper Drove and Station Road could be bought for around £10. Bungalows were the popular choice; they were relatively cheap and quick to build and provided a most acceptable home. Of course there was no sanitation, no plumbing and no electricity, but there was the luxury of a well which was sometimes shared.

Father built a number of these bungalows. They were timber framed and had a slated roof. They were clad with rebated, feathered-edge prepared weatherboard. The interior was lined with beaver-board or match-board, the former with covering strips. Two chimneys were built to provide a fireplace in all four rooms. There would be a passageway in the middle with a small cloakroom between the two rear rooms. The cost was around £200. They were popular with ex-servicemen. There were no mortgages available in those days.

Probably the last of these bungalows was built by father at the lower end of Station Road for Ted Whale, a policeman. It was recently demolished to make way for a large property. His wife Rose lived there until shortly before her passing. I have previously mentioned Wherwell-born Rose who worked with her uncle – Fred Young – at the dairy.

I watched some of the bungalow being dismantled, because the timber was in such good condition it was done piece-by-piece and saved. All the stud work was tenoned into the plates, top and bottom. The weatherboarding was also in excellent condition and this too was saved.

The timber in those days was of such good quality – it had to be. Much of it was yellow deal from Archangel, Russia – which had a lovely smell when being worked – and was not only good, but also cheap. It had to be to build bungalows at that price. Truck loads were delivered to our yard at Wherwell. I remember Sentinel steam wagons arriving with it.

Demolition of bungalow in 2004 – built by father in Station Road, Chilbolton for Edward Whale in the late 1920s.

To grace the doorway for charm and protection, porches were added to properties in Chilbolton (now Village Street), including Abbots Farm, Abbots Rest, Horseshoe Cottage and St Michael's Cottage.

A prime central area, opposite Chilbolton village shop, was another location for a similar style bungalow. It was built for a retired railway inspector, Charles Tibble. In order to save on costs he added his own style flat roofed kitchen to the south aspect, but required father to build a chimney stack for it and provide a kitchen range for heating and cooking. Also fitted for him was a Belfast cane glazed sink with a semi-rotary hand-pump piped to a well which was dug nearby. Prices then were – kitchen range £3.15s, sink 22/- (shillings) and pump £2. A connecting door to the bungalow was also provided. Charles Tibble used mostly second-hand material and I remember some railway sleepers being used. Usually the added outside toilets were 'Elsan' closets – the cost of these including 3-inch diameter ventilation pipe and cowl was £2.7s.6d.

In later years Mrs Wallis from Church Farm House, Chilbolton acquired the property for retirement and approached father for improvements. Made in the carpenter's shop the two elegant bay windows with transoms and fanlights replaced the smaller front facing windows. This feature gave a pleasing appearance to the frontage and provided more interior space and light. Also prepared in the carpenter's shop, a full length glass roofed verandah was added to the rear to provide protection from the elements, with a central pitched section over the doorway. For this a retaining wall was built with steps to access the garden. A cement faced concrete pathway provided a clean undercover walkway.

In 1939 my late wife's mother lived there until her passing. The top end of the garden provided an excellent view overlooking the Common and beyond. It was appropriately named 'Fair View'. To the left of the bungalow, nearer the road, could be seen the concrete footings on which the former Mission Hall was built. It was entranced separately from the road.

Bungalow built by father in Village Street, Chilbolton for Mr C Tibble in the early 1920s (pictured with added bay windows).

Rear aspect of Mr Tibble's bungalow – pictured with added verandah for Mrs Wallis.

Later the property was acquired by the Manor House, Newton Stacey for retirement purposes and the name 'Newton House' applied. Today it is a large modern property.

A substantial brick constructed bungalow was built in Coley Lane, near the Station Road turning, for Doctor Moore. A carriage-drive for access was cut through the roadside bank.

I still have two of father's builders' merchants catalogues, that which he mostly used was William Dibben & Sons Limited, Builders' Merchants and Wholesale Ironmongers, Southampton. It is from 1936 and is Catalogue No. 36 containing 614 pages. Every item listed is priced and superbly illustrated, the smaller items with reduced prices for larger quantities, with some boxed items in gross lots. The wording above the Terms and Condition of Business on page two quotes:

> *"Tis not in mortals to command success,*
> *But we'll do more Sempronius, we'll deserve it".*

Then at the foot of the page:
> *"It is not so much the price you pay for the goods you get that counts,*
> *It's the goods you get for the price you pay'.*

Before the company extended its business with branches at Winchester and Andover in the late twenties, both buildings were identical with a traditional shop frontage. I remember father telling me that Ebenezer Dibben travelled to Wherwell on horse back to solicit orders, such was the company's zest for business in those days, soon after the Great War.

There were various suppliers of material in the Southampton area, such as paint and wallpaper, etc which would be put on passenger train to Wherwell Station and arrive the day after ordering. Window glass was bought in wooden crates, each containing 10 sheets, packed in straw and measuring 5 feet x 4 feet. Putty was in 28 lb kegs, nails in one hundredweight sacks, priced from three shillings.

Living in Mount Cottage (opposite our Wherwell cottage) in later years was Colonel and Mrs Dumas. Father extended the cottage for them, adding two rooms at the north end. Joinery for this was made in the carpenter's shop and the work was done with just one man, Oscar Smart, who had worked for father for 15 years. When completed it blended in with the old to provide a perfect match. It is now a pretty and attractive cottage.

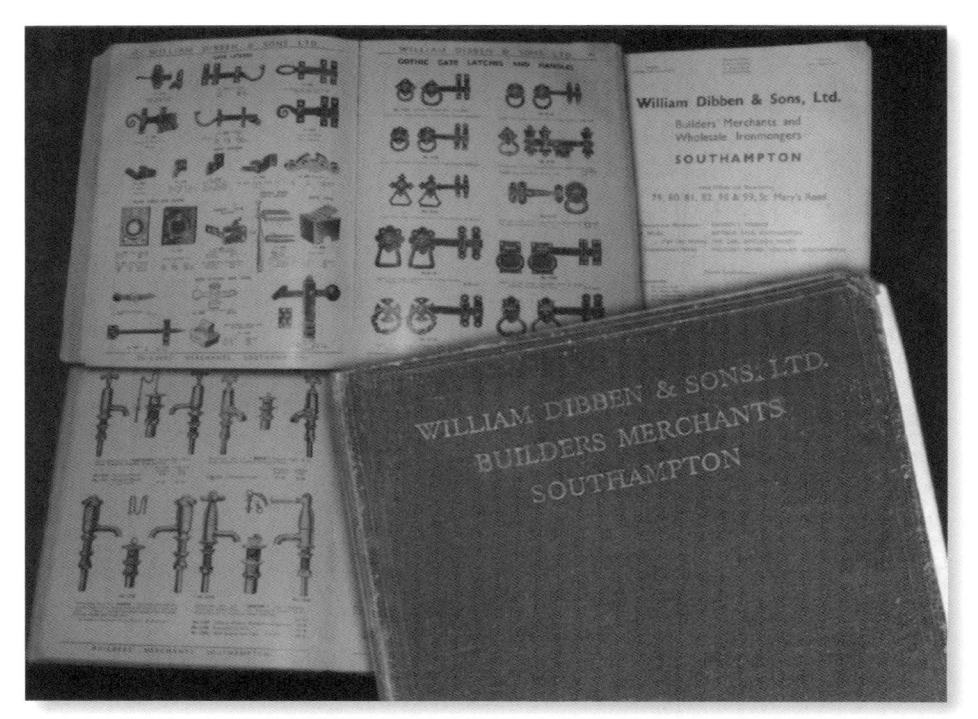

William Dibben and Sons Limited – Builders' Merchants Catalogue No. 36 issued 1936.

Just inside the boundary area of Mount Cottage, at the south-east corner, was once the site of another chalk-walled thatched cottage (part of it can be seen in the left-hand corner of one of the pictures in Chapter 1, its thatch line almost touching the hedge). It was probably entranced from New Barn Lane. As told by father, this too was thought to have been destroyed by fire with sparks from a passing train. If true, it does seem quite remarkable that Mount Cottage, and Mount View too, escaped such a similar fate. I often saw showers of sparks from the locomotives when ascending the steep gradient, especially with goods trains.

Colonel and Mrs Dumas had three children – Jeremy, Timothy and Nicola – and my wife's older sister was their nanny. The family required more living space and this was provided by father.

Charming Mount Cottage Wherwell extended by father in the early fifties.

Disaster on the Highway

A disastrous incident occurred with our lorry in 1927. Returning from Winchester with a full load of timber it broke down ascending the Andover Road hill. Macklin Bros (Ford Dealers from Andover) were called to the scene. Using a towing shaft with attached wheels (known as a towing dolly) placed under the front axle, it was towed back to Wherwell for unloading and then to Andover for repair. All was well until it approached the right-hand bend near the big bridge, Wherwell. Travelling too fast it overturned shedding its load. Probably induced by the reduced wheel width at the front end, which with its heavy load would cause it to sway. Macklin Bros had to pay for their carelessness.

Norman was with father. As there was not room for him in the cab, he had to be content with sitting on a box in the back of the towing vehicle. Before the driver approached the bend, Norman was banging on the rear view window shouting 'slow down, slow down'. The lorry was then swaying from side to side, but his plea went unheeded. Fortunately it fell on the grass verge which prevented serious damage. Transmission was always a problem with the Model 'T' Ford. It was actuated by depressing the left-hand foot pedal.

Destructive Conflagration

A bungalow built by father in Station Road was completely destroyed by fire but rebuilt within a matter of days. His workmen were there in force; it was another case of 'all hands to the pump'.

Another disastrous fire occurred at 'Testaway' in December 1925. A former well-known County cricketer, Mr H Martyn, was living there. The fire was so severe that only a few items of furniture were saved and only the walls were left standing. Getting water from the river was a problem in those days.

Father was given the task of rebuilding the property. He knew the architect and was fortunate to obtain a duplicate set of plans. It was rebuilt to the original specification which included a viewing balcony, a noticeable feature of the property.

Another fire broke out in November 1950 at the village shop, Chilbolton when Mrs Hunt was awakened by a loud explosion and found one of her two petrol pumps blazing furiously. The fire was confined to the top of the pump, which was sealed off from the storage tank; it burnt itself out before the fire brigade arrived. In earlier years when it was only one pump I remember father buying petrol there for his first car. A measured gallon was hand pumped into a cylindrical shaped glass container at the head of the pump. A lever in the nozzle of the hose controlled release. The price then was 2/6d for two gallons.

Other Building Works

Previously at Newton House, Colonel Lloyd acquired Rooksbury Mill, Andover and lived in the mill house. He wanted the mill converted into a dance hall and entrusted the work to father. For this undertaking the river was dammed to gain access to the huge waterwheel, the removal of which, together with the shafting and machinery, was difficult and heavy work. Once removed, a stage was constructed. The hall was built with a balcony at each side, an added feature of the transformation. A new floor was laid of pine tongued and grooved boarding which was secretly nailed (I still have a piece). When completed it was full of character, a unique venue for house parties.

I always enjoyed going there with father in our lorry. To get to it we had to cross the railway which was just a few yards from the mill; the crossing gates were always closed. The gatekeeper lived in the cottage alongside the line but first had to ring the signal box at Andover Town Station for permission to open the gates to let us through. Sometimes a train was due and that was always interesting for me, but not for father!

In 1927 a piece of land in Wherwell, accessed from New Barn Lane, was acquired by an artist, Ernest Fox from Surrey. The bungalow built for him was of timber construction with rebated weather-board cladding. Owing to the contour of the area ground work was required to produce a level site and this was all done by hand. The bungalow was centrally heated, the radiators piped to a kitchen range fitted with a high-pressure boiler. It was not entirely efficient due to the 10 feet high ceilings. There were no fireplaces. Father used his divining skill to source water supply for the bungalow where, with the use of ladders, ropes and buckets, a well was dug to a depth of 62 feet by two of his workmen in just one week – no hard hats then. (Both lived in Wherwell, one I remember was Bert Horne.) The earth removed was used to raise the ground level where the studio was erected, which arrived in sections from his previous address and was reassembled.

A substantial, spacious house was built in 1928 on land adjoining and owned by my grandparents at their shop in Fullerton Road. An attractive balcony, entranced by French doors from the first floor extended to the full width of the house and provided an excellent view of the river and beyond. A well was dug for water supply and piped to a hand-pump in the utility room. The bricks used for the building were supplied by the Bursledon Brick Company and railed to Wherwell Station. I helped father unload – usually three bricks with each throw.

Father's work was also evident in churches at Wherwell, Chilbolton and Leckford. In 1897, to mark the Diamond Jubilee of Queen Victoria, a Jubilee weather wane was placed on top of the church steeple in Chilbolton. However in 1927 a severe gale dislodged the weather vane and shaft from its fixing and appeared to be in danger of falling. Because of this the church was temporarily closed. Father acted quickly – wooden scaffolding, from our yard nearby, was erected up to and around the tower, with ladders lashed to the rear of the spire to reach the shaft. Secured by ropes, the heavy shaft was safely lowered to the ground and removed to the carpenter's shop for restoration and painting. A new oak capping block was made and fitted to the apex of the spire and the shaft assembly refitted. This was

A recent photograph of Chilbolton Church depicts that after 80 years the weather vane and shaft, repaired and restored to the spire by father in 1927, is still perpendicular.

quite a hazardous undertaking in those days. I remember father telling me that special insurance was arranged to cover the risks involved. The clock face and tower were repainted at the same time. At Leckford Church a new chancel screen and organ loft were installed.

Funereal Duties

But there was more to father's caring attitude, for he also was the village undertaker and funeral director, not only for Wherwell, Chilbolton and Fullerton, but also for other villages too. He was much respected for his kindness and sympathy at such a difficult time when families were grieving. In the early twenties the usual practice was to use the bier (a four-wheeled hand frame to carry a coffin), which was kept in the church, to convey the coffin from the deceased's cottage to the church. Later Mr S Halcrow from Andover supplied a hearse, which then had seating for the

Interior of Leckford Church showing the new Choir Stalls and Organ Chamber erected by father in 1925. In later years I was privileged to play the organ. *(courtesy of Brian Fakes)*

Father in his funeral attire

Building Business prior to Father

In the latter part of the nineteenth century and into the early part of the twentieth century the building business was located in Fullerton Road and run by William (Bill) Spratt's father, Albert Spratt. An area of land sited beyond May Cottage was his builder's yard. It was fronted at the roadside with a period single storey chalk walled thatched building. Behind it was a saw-pit, over which heavy timber and tree trunks would be sawn by two men – one standing below and the other above the timber. For this work they used a large two-handed cross-cut saw, six feet in length.

four bearers. All the coffins, mostly of elm and oak, were made in the carpenter's shop. I assisted with this work, even before I left school. For many years the cost of a funeral was less than £20; for the very poor it was just a few pounds, sometimes nothing. I still have father's top hat (used for funerals) in its original box. A life-long resident in Chilbolton once said to me "your father was Mr Chilbolton". I was touched with such a nice compliment. In later years, caskets for cremation funerals were acquired from London – by rail.

A special birthday celebration for father in 1967, dressed as requested in his funeral attire by local retired businessmen from Wherwell and Chilbolton on the occasion of their annual lunch at the Abbotts Mitre.

The pit was probably some six feet square and of similar depth. It was hard and arduous work, both for the man pushing the saw and the other pulling. Muscular strong men were required and Wherwell could supply.

There was a number of open fronted cart sheds with corrugated galvanised iron cladding, which was also used for roof coverings. In addition there were stables for his horses and several timber built sheds. It was from one or two of these that Mr Thompson made his 'Wherwell Cars' in 1921/22.

Mr A G Prangley (known as George) lived with his wife and daughter in the small cottage adjoining Bill Spratt's builder's office. George worked for Bill Spratt and later became self-employed. He used a motorcycle and side-car for transport and employed an assistant – he occupied the side-car. In the early thirties George built a bungalow in Coley Lane, Chilbolton and resided there on completion. Mrs Holder later occupied his Wherwell dwelling.

Chapter 7

Duty in War and Peace

Royal Navy

At school with me was Richard John (known as Jack) Trowbridge. His father, Albert Trowbridge, was a local farmer; the family lived at Manor Farm House, Wherwell and I often played there with him. At 12 years of age Jack attended Andover Grammar School. With farming in the doldrums he left school at 15 (1935) to join the Royal Navy. He was commissioned in 1940 and served at sea throughout the Second World War.

My uncle, Chief Petty Officer Henry Blackall, served at sea during the Great War.

This is just a brief account of Jack's phenomenal success in his distinguished naval career spanning 40 years, from boy sailor to Rear Admiral Sir Richard Trowbridge, and from boy sailor to Flag Officer and Captain of the *Royal Yacht Britannia*, also the last Briton to serve as Governor of Western Australia.

Sir Richard was torpedoed aboard the battleship *Barham* in November 1941. He took part in the North African, Sicilian and Italian landings and also served in the Far East. At the end of

My uncle, Reginald Irving (known as Irving) Blackall, served at sea during the Great War.

hostilities with Japan he was in the destroyer *Wakeful* and transported prisoners of war to Sydney. In this operation he was mentioned in dispatches. This also was the time he met HRH Prince Philip, who was First Lieutenant of another destroyer in the 27th Destroyer Flotilla. Together they were in Tokyo Bay when the Japanese signed their surrender after atomic bombs had been dropped on Hiroshima and Nagasaki.

After the War other appointments followed, whilst as staff gunnery officer in Singapore he met and married his wife. Their passage home as passengers was interrupted by the Suez crisis which meant they were forced to enjoy a second honeymoon on a troopship which diverted them via the Cape.

Richard (Jack) Trowbridge with his sister Enid and younger brother Kenneth at their Wherwell Manor Farm home in the 1930s. *(courtesy of Margaret Trowbridge, sister-in-law)*

As Commander Trowbridge he captained the destroyer *Carysfort* in the Mediterranean from 1956-1958, then served as the second-in-command of the cruiser *Bermuda* 1958-59 before returning to the gunnery school at Whale Island at Portsmouth where he was promoted to Captain. In a later appointment he was to command the guided missile destroyer *Hampshire* which for many years was the flagship of the Western Fleet.

But Captain Trowbridge also had an unusually long-serving and successful term as Flag Officer Royal Yachts from 1970 to 1975 when *Britannia* was enjoying one of her busiest periods. He energetically entered into proposals to take *Britannia* on long trips with HM The Queen and HRH Prince Philip to Vancouver for the Royal visit. In 1974 *Britannia* was touring the Pacific and the Indian Oceans until the Queen had to return home when Edward Heath's Conservative Government lost the General Election. Captain Trowbridge continued in his task, taking Prince Philip on to Australia.

Five years later the Western Australian government experienced some difficulty in finding a suitable Australian for the post of Governor of Western Australia – the answer was Rear Admiral Sir Richard Trowbridge.

His home was Idsworth in Hampshire. For more than 30 years a stalwart member of his parish at the Anglo Saxon church of St Hubert's. It was unfortunate that his life was overshadowed by exposure to asbestos which was being removed from *Britannia* during a long refit which he supervised. He died on 4 May 2003. He was appointed KCVO in 1983.

I am indebted to Jack's brother Ken and his wife Margaret for their help in compiling this tribute. Since writing this, sadly Ken has passed away.

Rear Admiral Sir Richard Trowbridge.
(courtesy of Margaret Trowbridge, sister-in-law)

(The above text includes extracts from the Obituaries column in the Daily Telegraph dated 9 May 2003.)

Army

Alfred John Parker (chauffeur to Colonel and Mrs A E Jenkins at Wherwell Priory) was a volunteer and enlisted in the Army at the outbreak of the Great War in 1914 and served as a Motor Transport Driver in the Army Service Corps – his Regimental Number was 031635. He was sent to France on 18 March 1915 and served with various units. Alfred was demobilised

My uncle, Frederick Blackall, in uniform during the Great War.

in early 1919 having been awarded three medals; he was proud to have served God, King and Country. Alfred Parker, elder son of Alfred John Parker, served in the Second Great War, he was mobilised into the Corps of Royal Engineers – his Regimental Number was 14653403. Alfred (known as Bert) was promoted Sergeant and posted to India in May 1944; he was demobilised early 1946.

The photograph (seen earlier) of Vera, with her fiancé Cecil (known as Bob) Gambrill (a former Grammar School pupil) was taken before the War. They married in 1940 on his Conscription into the Pioneer Corps. He had been rejected in 1939 as being short-sighted.

Alfred John Parker, a volunteer, served throughout the Great War.
(courtesy of Laurie Parker)

Commissioned from Sergeant in 1941 and following service in Glasgow he was selected to command a newly raised company of Bechuana Soldiers stationed in Haifa whose duties included defence of the port and refinery areas, coupled with detachment duties on similar installations in Beirut and Tripoli.

He was subsequently promoted Commanding Officer of 57 Group Pioneer Corps responsible for garrison and other duties pending the arrival of reinforcements from the United Kingdom and covering Southern Palestine. He was released in 1946 and granted the honorary rank of Lieutenant Colonel.

Bob's pre war working life was with the Andover Co-operative Society and he studied at the Co-operative Union's Education Department gaining Managerial and Related Diplomas. Following Military Service he was recruited to the Colonial Service as an Assistant Registrar of Co-operative Societies in the Gold Coast (now Ghana). My sister joined him in Africa and the work that was of a judicial and training nature involved extensive travelling in the Colony and Ashanti to establish a Co-operative Movement centred on Cocoa Farming but also expanding to retail trading, banking and village utility services. Vera accompanied

Bob on trek and from the age of six months their daughter Jane travelled with them. The long blond 'pig tails' of a fair young child caused great interest among the village women who begged to be allowed to touch them. Government Rest House accommodation was rudimentary with a constant need to be on guard against visiting snakes, scorpions, swarms of ants or even goats in the kitchen.

The family returned to the United Kingdom in 1957 after the Colony gained independence as Ghana.

It was in Accra that Vera acquired the skill in creating some fine specimens of marquetry, the process of inlaying wood with designs of coloured wood. Like her mother, Vera was an accomplished organist and played at the village church where they later lived. Another quality was dressmaking and in later years she made all her own clothes. At one period Vera did all the alterations for a local ladies dress shop. Yet there was more, it was Vera's magic touch with the artist's brush to capture the scene at Winchester Corner, Wherwell - produced from the riverside inside the Priory Park. Another painting was of the village street looking north from Pound Tree Green.

Mahogany elephant table and baby elephant bought in West Africa by Vera for mother.

The following two verses are a tribute to my sister:

The Evergreen Lady, my sister I treasure,
So gifted and talented, it is beyond measure,
In the home, in the garden, her floral displays,
Her skill at the organ, a joy to hear,
Our favourite hymns we loved so dear.

Then there's the needlework, itself a profession,
Designed and fashioned by her skill,
So many fine garments, her wardrobe did fill,
Her artistic flair with the artists brush,
Brings memories back of Winchester Corner.

Marquetry work by Vera.

Winchester Corner, Wherwell by Vera.

Wherwell near Pound Tree Green by Vera.

At the start of the Second World War Victor Pyke was called up for military service in the Army and posted to the 2nd Battalion of the Wiltshire Regiment. After training at Devizes he was sent to Scotland. Later he was moved to Liverpool and Ireland. After an illness in Ireland, which put him in hospital, Victor was posted to the 7th Battalion and involved in sea defence work around Milford-on-Sea and Highcliffe. Eventually he was to serve as a replacement to the 2nd Battalion, where he served in Suez, Palestine, Syria, Damascus, France and finishing up in Hanover where he was demobbed and returned to Wherwell.

On his return home Victor assisted his father and later in 1947 took over the tenancy of the White Lion when his father retired. Sadly Victor passed away in October 2008.

Also at school with me was Jim Lewis, the family lived in the end cottage on Fullerton Road. Sadly Jim died whilst in Japanese captivity when serving in Burma.

Another pupil was Ernest Nutley, the family lived in what was known as the Woodman's Cottage near the Pound Tree. Sadly he lost his life whilst on active service.

Walter Smith was just 14 years of age when his father, Harry Smith, succeeded Mr Hand as the village blacksmith at Wherwell in 1934. The family lived in Forge Cottage.

Walter was called up for National Service in the early part of the Second Great War and served with the Royal Sussex Battalion, 133 Brigade. His regiment, with many others, was drafted to the Middle East Forces and fought at the battle of Egypt, 23 October-9 November 1942.

It was on the vital northern sector of the 40 miles front, some 15 miles from El Alamein, that Walter was engaged in the great battle at Kidney Ridge – the strongest point in the enemy line. The infantry breakthrough had taken nine days of hard fighting. On 2 November the Allied mighty tank force hurled through the gap in the line like a thunderbolt and just a few miles on at Tell El Aqqaqir (the Hill of the Wicked) to the west of Kidney Ridge, a violent tank battle raged for some nine hours between the opposing armour. The pace was terrific, the enemy proved unable to stand the strain. The battle was to finish Rommel's army. By 5 November some 260 enemy tanks had been destroyed, the desert battleground was a cemetery of enemy tanks. By 8 November no enemy forces of any importance were left in Egypt. (Rommel had 12 divisions – perhaps 100,000 men against 10 Allied divisions.)

Walter survived the battle but sadly many of his comrades were killed in action. In the battle for Egypt the 8th Army had suffered a loss of some 13,600 officers and men. Sadly too Walter is no longer with us for he passed away on 14 June 2005. His son Darrell now occupies Forge Cottage. Walter was a good friend and neighbour and much respected.

Major Charles Liddell of Fullerton joined the Army Rifle Brigade in 1937 and served in India for two years. Charles spent much of the Second Great War in the North African Campaign fighting in the Western Desert, where he was awarded the Military Cross, one of the first to be awarded in the war for his bravery in finding a safe path through the enemy's deadly minefield; so vital for the success of the Allied advance. Major Liddell also arrested Himmler's brother towards the end of the war. (It is quite possible that Major Liddell was in the same area of the vital northern sector of the front – the strongest point in the enemy line - where Walter Smith was engaged in the fighting.)

Royal Air Force

Norman, my brother, joined the Royal Air Force in 1935 and rose from Airman to the rank of Squadron Leader. His initial training was at the Royal Air Force Establishment, Uxbridge, after which his first posting was to Andover Royal Air Force Station where his flying training commenced. All the aircraft then were bi-planes with open cockpits. Norman also trained as a wireless operator, flying the Vickers Virginia twin-engined night bomber aircraft. A posting to Boscombe Down followed and in 1938/39 it was to Norfolk for radar installation work off the Norfolk coast. Shortly after the outbreak of the Second World War he was posted to Egypt.

Deserts have always been associated with a particular peril, that of being stranded in their midst without sufficient food or water. Pilots and aircrew knew this only too well, many contrived with great courage and endurance to walk back to their squadron, often piercing the enemy lines in order to do so. But the chief torment was the dust storms, thick as a dense London fog, which ripped down tents, covered everything with grit, made flying impossible and might last for hours.

Huge bombproof stores and repair shops were set up in the caves in the Mokattan Hills, south of Cairo. A formidable air power was built up to defeat the enemy, an air force of the United Nations working under the operational control of the Royal Air Force. But it had not always been powerful, for in June 1940 the Royal Air Force faced almost impossible odds with a handful of squadrons flying into battle in obsolescent aircraft; nevertheless, on most occasions they held the enemy out of the air.

The War in the Middle East was a struggle for airfields. The North African Campaigns were to last for three years. On 16 May 1943 when the last enemy cleansing was done in Tunisia, the Axis powers, ie Italy and Germany, had been 'hit for six' out of Africa. It was a victorious end to the campaign in which the Axis had lost 7,600 aircraft.

Norman at home whilst on leave from duty at RAF Station, Andover in 1935 (the uniform worn then was much the same as in the Great War).

After the North African Campaign victory, He returned to the United Kingdom (UK) in the troopship *Devonshire*, one of a convoy of ships sailing in line ahead – so close that they almost touched. It was so overloaded that men had to sleep in gangways, in fact anywhere they could find space for a mattress. The ship docked in the Clyde.

Egypt 1941 - Norman in fatigue-dress with his right-hand man.

The troopship *Devonshire*.

After the War he was posted to various Royal Air Force stations in the UK, among them Henlow, Waterbeach (twice) and Waddington. In 1948 he was involved in the Berlin Airlift flying Dakota aircraft. In the 1950/60s there were two postings to Headquarters, Royal Air Force, Germany. He attended officer training courses at the Royal Air Force College, Cranwell and had a long spell of duty at the Air Ministry, London

A Royal Air Force custom – officers wait on the sergeants (and wives) on Christmas Day. Norman *(pictured right)* on such an occasion at RAF Headquarters, Cologne, Germany after the war.

Norman taking the salute at an inspection parade at RAF Station, Henlow.

Norman retired in September 1966 and lived with his wife at Ferndown, Dorset. He died on 19 October 2003.

I am proud to write this brief tribute to Norman for he was my guiding hand through life.

Soon after the outbreak of war in 1939, my late wife's older sister Kate was called up for National Service and joined the Women's Royal Air Force. After training at a Royal Air Force Nursing College, Kate was posted to hospital nursing duties and during the Battle of Britain served at coastal RAF Stations nursing and caring for wounded airmen. Before and after the war she, too, was an officers' nanny. In later years Kate was a school nurse at a private school in Basingstoke.

Raymond Parker, elder son of Mr and Mrs Archie Parker and grandson of Alfred John Parker, was brought up in Wherwell. Always keen on flying, he joined the Air Training Corps after leaving school. Ray enlisted in the Royal Air Force on 6 January 1943 (Service Number 1851671) and was posted to No. 14 Initial Training Wing

My Royal Air Force column in tribute to Norman.

as a member of the RAF Volunteer Reserve as an aircrafthand under training for Air Gunner aircrew duties. Later he was posted to No. 1 Elementary Air Gunner School, and on 4 December 1943 was selected to attend No. 90 Air Gunner's Course at RAF Pembry. Awarded Air Gunner's Brevet, Ray was promoted Sergeant on 27 January 1944 and transferred to No. 290 Aircrew Training Unit in February 1944. Finally on 24 May 1944 posted to No. 1660 Conversion Unit, RAF Swinderby, Lincolnshire for final training as an operational crew member flying Short Stirling 4-engined aircraft. The Stirling ranked as the most powerful and heaviest military machine then in service, with great offensive powers and also for its defensive qualities with great fire power furnished by its multi-gun turrets. It weighed 30 tons and carried bombs weighing nearly a ton (probably then the pride of Bomber Command). Ray manned the swivelling rear gun turret. (Conversion Unit: training and preparation of flying crews for operational duties.)

Sergeant Raymond Parker, killed on active service 1944. *(courtesy of Laurie Parker)*

Sadly it was later to end in disaster for on 24 July 1944 the Mk.III Stirling, in which Ray was flying on a training flight in the United Kingdom, crashed and burst into flames, killing all nine crew members. Ray died on active service for his country. It was a tragic end for such a young life.

It was a bitter blow for his father, for only recently he had lost his wife from a terminal illness. This double tragedy left him distraught and distressed. The anguish each day as the weeks and months passed by was a heavy burden to bear. But hope springs eternal, out of despair and sadness brighter days were to come that would cheer his way and restore confidence in his life.

With a little encouragement Archie re-married, his new bride was Margaret Taylor - a 'lady-in-waiting' with professional nanny skills. The wedding took place at St Mary the Less Church, Chilbolton on 30 March 1948.

In May 1949 Archie and Margaret became proud parents of a son and Raymond was a middle name.

Notwithstanding the dreadful tragedy in which Ray was killed, a compelling interest persuaded Ray's younger brother Adrian to follow in his footsteps, for when leaving school he too joined the Andover Air Training Corps. Later in 1950, when called up for National Service, Adrian also enlisted in the Royal Air Force and was stationed at RAF Padgate, in Lancashire, for initial training. Following this he was posted to RAF Station Melksham for trade training as an aircraft electrician/mechanic. Adrian was finally posted to RAF Station Lyneham (which was nearer home) and from there was discharged in December 1952. Adrian now lives in Devizes, where I regularly keep in touch with him.

The way it was – Margaret, my sister-in-law (the officers' nanny) with two of her charges in the 1930s.

The wedding of Archie and Margaret Parker with bridesmaids and his brother Bert.

'Bevin's Boys'

During the Second Great War Mr Ernest Bevin, Minister of State for Energy, introduced an order directing men called up for military service into coal mining – this was necessary to maintain the coal mining strength, so vital to the nation. Those selected, which was by ballot, were called 'Bevin's Boys' and received the Bevin Boys' Badge with the citation:

'Presented in recognition of your valuable contribution to the war effort.'
Signed: Ernest Bevin,
Minister of State for Energy.

Known to me are Ken Trowbridge (mentioned earlier and now deceased) and Frank Cooper (my cousin who lives at Landford).

Adrian Parker, member of the Air Training Corp and later the Royal Air Force.

Army Auxiliary Workshops

I attended a medical examination in Salisbury on 28 May 1940 for National Service and was placed in Grade four. This was because of my chest complaint which exempted me from military service but not war service. During the war period from 1939 the company I worked for, Anna Valley Motors (Andover) Limited, under a Ministry of Supply Contract, became an Army Auxiliary Workshop, and in this capacity operated as one of the few points in the south where repairs to a large variety of service vehicles could be undertaken. At one point during hostilities no less than 13 different makes of vehicles were undergoing repairs simultaneously, and of the hundreds of vehicles repaired, not a single vehicle failed to pass the most searching test which followed every repair operation.

World War 1914-19 – Peace Celebration Mug.

Government War-time publications in 1939.

War-time gas mask – fortunately never used.

Together with my other clerical duties I was responsible for the costing work involved.

An Inspector regularly attended our works, he was probably based at Taskers – then producing the 'Queen Mary' type trailers, used for salvaging crashed aircraft. My wife's elder sister Margaret was drafted there for War work and was on the production line for these trailers.

Our Salisbury branch, Anna Valley Motors (Salisbury) Limited in Castle Street, was also requisitioned when the Spitfire factory in Southampton was bombed. Here complete wing production for the fighter planes was undertaken and many hundreds were made by the end of the war and was after work.

A splendid war effort by the company in the country's time of need.

Dedication of the Great War Memorial in 1922 by the Reverend B C Taylor, then Vicar of Wherwell.

Chapter 8

Transport

Buses

The first bus to operate through the villages was a Model 'T' Ford. It was fitted with a wooden box type body with side windows and could seat five passengers either side; entrance was at the rear via steps. A roof rack was provided for the luggage.

The vehicle was owned by Mr Prince, licensee at the New Inn, Chilbolton, and was called the 'Ropley'. He had previously lived in that village, hence the name. It only operated on Fridays for market days for Chilbolton and Wherwell. The fare was 1s 0d (one shilling).

Chevrolet 14-seater 'all-weather' coach, with happy day trippers aboard.
It could be Sam Robinson's 'Kiaora' and pictured by him, circa 1927.

Later, Mr Sam Robinson of The Drove, Chilbolton acquired a new Chevrolet 14-seater, all-weather coach with a foldaway hood and side curtains. It was called the 'Kiaora' and also operated on Fridays for market days; he also used it for private hire work.

The next operator was The Andover and District Motor Services, set up by Mr Herbert Wolstenholme and his son Derek from Houghton. (Derek was always popular with the passengers.) Their route was Andover, Stockbridge and Romsey, via Wherwell, Longstock, Houghton and King's Somborne. A regular daily service operated using 14-seater Chevrolet buses. As passenger traffic increased, a new 20-seater Dennis bus was added in 1929. The return fare from Wherwell to Andover was 6d (old coinage).

New buses for Andover & District Motor Services. 20-seater Dennis UL 9607, acquired in March 1929. 20-seater Guy UK 8818, acquired in March 1930. Pictured here with proprietor Herbert Wolstenholme and his son Derek. *(courtesy of the David Pennels Collection)*

At its commencement the service operated via Fullerton Road, with a U-turn being made at The White Lion for its onward journey to Stockbridge. This was very convenient for people living in the area, but they were soon to lose the service as it was to be re-routed through Wherwell and Chilbolton. It then became a somewhat circuitous route for Stockbridge and Longstock passengers, but more profitable with the extra traffic it generated.

Some buses were routed via Clatford and approached Andover via Barlows Lane. Because there was little traffic on the roads in those days passengers could board the bus close to where they lived. There were no official bus stops.

In 1929 Venture Limited, based in Basingstoke, was already operating regular daily services to Andover via Whitchurch and Longparish (its premier route). The company now entered the race with a daily service from Andover to Stockbridge which followed the same route as Andover and District Motor Services. Venture used a 20-seater Thornycroft bus with a uniformed crew. A bus conductor in those days was a plus for passengers; they liked it and so did I.

Thornycroft 20-seater bus, similar to that used for the Andover-Stockbridge service, seen here during a heavy thunderstorm – almost like the river Test. *(courtesy of John Pearce)*

Competition became fierce, the frequency and timings were such that Venture and Andover and District both left their Stockbridge termini at approximately the same time. The bus in front would stop in the middle of the road to pick up passengers so as to prevent its rival passing. Drivers of Andover and District Motor Services had to collect fares whilst Venture could do this on the move with a bus conductor.

The Venture bus was out-stationed at Stockbridge, but the service only lasted a matter of months. It did seem to have provoked Andover and District Motor Services into placing several advertisements in the Andover Advertiser. The reason the service came to rather an abrupt end was, I understand, a shortage of vehicles at Basingstoke where the need was greatest.

It is interesting to note that Venture Limited was launched only three years earlier on 1 May 1926 with just three vehicles, two days before the General Strike. By 1929 the fleet had risen to 14 vehicles and they were operating around 14 services in the Basingstoke area. With little or no reserve for emergencies one can understand why the Stockbridge service came to a sudden end. It must have been a difficult decision to make but prestige in the main area of operation was paramount.

Andover and District Motor Services was back in control. In 1930, to further improve the service, Mr Wolstenholme acquired a further new 20-seater bus. This time it was a Guy which featured a semi-forward enclosed driver's cab. (Unusual for its size as normally this type of construction was for the larger 32-seater class, as with the Leyland Lion.) It was the company's flagship – but not for long, for there was worse to come, much worse.

On 10 May 1930 Wilts and Dorset Motor Services Limited, then rapidly expanding in the Andover area, commenced a daily service to Romsey, using the same route as Andover and District Motor Services, with the introduction of its larger Leyland Lion 32-seater rear loading buses and uniformed personnel. A bus stop was included at Horsebridge Station for railway passengers.

I was at the dairy and recall seeing the first 'Lion' bus enter the village. Though just a boy I was impressed by its size and smartness. Compared with the little Chevrolets it was a goliath.

Twenty-five bus stops with fare stages and timetables were erected along the route. Passengers were then expected to board at these points; there was to be no casual picking up along the way. This was a safety measure and saved time. The first timetable boards were headed:

Wilts & Dorset Motor Services Limited
(In association with the Southern Railway)

Wilts and Dorset quickly won over passengers with its larger buses and friendly conductors. It was nice to find a seat before paying the fare. It was a clean, reliable and efficient service; the frequency was approximately two-hourly with additional buses for market days and weekends. The last bus terminated at Stockbridge, where it was out-stationed.

Such was the concern of Andover and District Motor Services that a letter quickly appeared in its glass faced timetable display case calling for loyalty from its passengers. The company had put in the spadework to build up the service and in return had pleaded for support to continue. It was a desperate appeal, but sadly it was a losing battle – it had to end. Mr Wolstenholme had no alternative but to sell his Andover and District Motor Bus Services to Wilts and Dorset Motor Services within a matter of days. (A timetable display case was affixed to the wall at Fred Young's dairy – a designated boarding/alighting point.)

The Wilts and Dorset Motor Services office was then at 29 High Street, Andover, opposite the Guildhall. A waiting room was provided for passengers. Such was the increase in passenger traffic that the larger buses were frequently filled to capacity and we often had to stand. Relief buses were provided at weekends. The company, part of the Tilling Group, had the capacity to do this, whereas the Andover and District bus had to return to collect the waiting passengers that had been left behind. An efficient parcels service was provided by the company. For Wherwell these were left at the Twentieth Century Stores.

The return fare from Wherwell to Andover increased by 2d to 8d. Workmen's return fare was at a single fare rate of 5d issued before 9.00 am. Passengers quickly became friendly with the bus crews and I still remember the following drivers: George Plowman, Frank Cannings,

New from 1928 the first Leyland Lion 32-seater bus to operate the Wilts & Dorset, Andover-Romsey service, via Wherwell and Chilbolton in May 1930. They were mostly replaced in 1938 by the more progressive, stylish and comfortable Leyland Tiger Series. *(courtesy of the David Pennels Collection)*

Dick May (ex Andover and District) and Derek Wolstenholme. Among the conductors were Jack White, Ted Sivier and Arthur Cole. Some stayed with the company until retirement.

There was a downside for the drivers with the Leyland buses; they were not fitted with self-starters and had to be cranked by hand – no easy task in Stockbridge in cold frosty weather! When severe, the radiator had to be drained and refilled in the morning with water dipped from the river stream at the opposite side of the street. Antifreeze was not then available.

Another operator for a short period of time was Horne's Coaches of Andover.

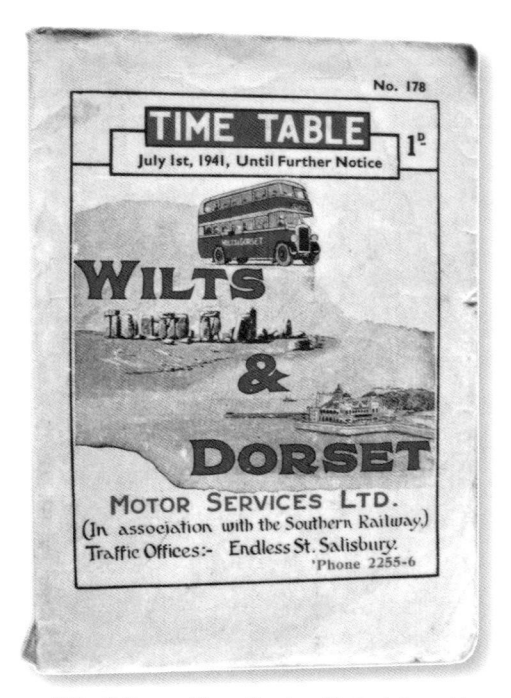

Wilts & Dorset Motor Services Limited timetable booklet, price 1d. Used when a part-time bus conductor for the company during the war.

Highways – Work by Father

In 1930 the road from Wherwell to Chilbolton was opened up where the brook stream flowed under it. A new culvert was created to carry the stream and at a lower level to eliminate the hump in the road. It was closed for three days. (The Wilts and Dorset buses were re-routed via Newton Stacey crossroads.) During the excavation work father discovered a cow bell. After a clean up it hung from the oak beam in our living room.

Railways

Much has already been written about the line from Hurstbourne to Fullerton with stations at Longparish and Wherwell. However, I think it is appropriate to include a brief introduction and history of the line for the benefit of newcomers to our villages.

Looking down from the Mount showing the London and South Western Railway in the early 1900s.

Wherwell Station with uniform staff in early LSWR days. Note the long platforms. *(courtesy of Lens of Sutton)*

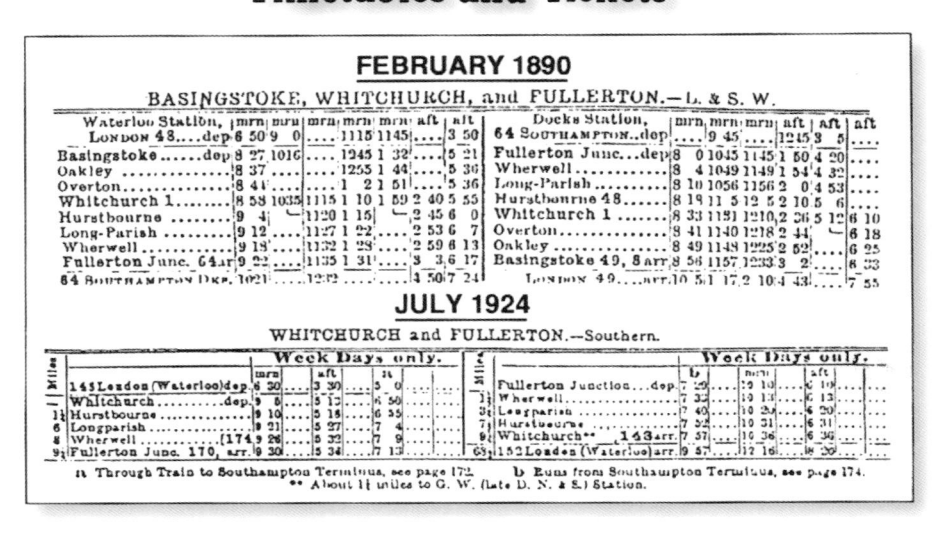

Timetables and Tickets

FEBRUARY 1890
BASINGSTOKE, WHITCHURCH, and FULLERTON.—L. & S. W.

Waterloo Station, London 48 ....dep	mrn 6 50	mrn 9 0	mrn	mrn 1115	mrn 1145	aft	aft 3 50	Docks Station, 64 Southampton..dep	mrn	mrn 9 45	mrn	aft 1245	aft 3 5	aft ....
Basingstoke......dep	8 27	1016	....	1245	1 32	....	5 21	Fullerton Junc...dep	8 0	1045	1145	1 50	4 20	....
Oakley	8 37	....	....	1255	1 44	....	5 36	Wherwell.............	8 4	1049	1149	1 54	4 32	....
Overton.............	8 44	....	....	1 2	1 51	....	5 36	Long-Parish.........	8 10	1056	1156	2 0	4 53	....
Whitchurch 1......	8 53	1035	1115	1 10	1 59	2 40	5 55	Hurstbourne 48...	8 19	11 5	12 5	2 10	5 6	....
Hurstbourne	9 4	....	1120	1 15	—	2 45	6 0	Whitchurch 1......	8 33	1151	1210	2 36	5 12	6 10
Long-Parish	9 12	....	1127	1 22	....	2 53	6 7	Overton.............	8 41	1140	1218	2 44	—	6 18
Wherwell............	9 18	....	1132	1 29	....	2 59	6 13	Oakley	8 49	1148	1225	2 52	....	6 25
Fullerton Junc. 64 arr	9 22	....	1135	1 31	....	3 3	6 17	Basingstoke 49, 8 arr	8 56	1157	1233	3 2	....	6 33
64 Southampton Dks.	1021	....	12:2	....	....	3 50	7 24	London 49......arr	10 51	17.2	10 4	43	....	7 55

JULY 1924
WHITCHURCH and FULLERTON.—Southern.

		Week Days only.							Week Days only.		
Miles		mrn	aft				Miles		mrn	mrn	aft
—	145 London (Waterloo) dep	6 30	3 30	5 0	....	....	—	Fullerton Junction...dep	7 29	9 10	6 10
—	Whitchurch......dep	9 5	5 12	6 50	....	....	1½	Wherwell.............	7 32	10 13	6 13
1½	Hurstbourne	9 10	5 18	6 55	....	....	3	Longparish	7 40	10 24	6 20
6	Longparish	9 21	5 27	7 4	....	....	7	Hurstbourne.........	7 52	10 31	6 31
8	Wherwell......[174	9 26	5 32	7 9	....	....	9	Whitchurch**...143 arr	7 57	10 36	6 36
9	Fullerton Junc. 170, arr	9 30	5 34	7 13	....	....	63	152 London (Waterloo) arr	9 57	12 16	8 39

a Through Train to Southampton Terminus, see page 172.   b Runs from Southampton Terminus, see page 174.
** About 1¼ miles to G. W. (late D. N. & S.) Station.

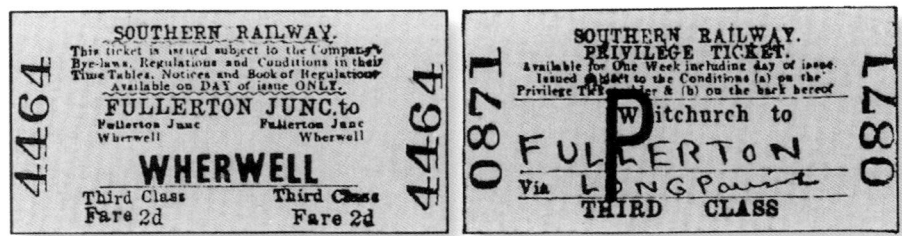

Tickets from the G.R.Croughton Collection.

Timetables and tickets. *(courtesy of Lens of Sutton)*

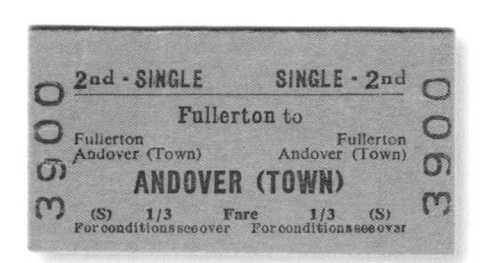

A second class single ticket Fullerton to Andover (Town).

Wherwell Railway Station showing the canopied entrance, balustrade and dormer window.
(courtesy of Lens of Sutton)

The original reason for building the line was to offer an alternative through route to the one planned by the Didcot, Newbury and Southampton Railway, which, having reached Newbury, wanted to continue its line south via Whitchurch to Southampton. With plans for a connection between the two companies at Whitchurch, the London and South Western Railway felt that the Hurstbourne to Fullerton Railway would also give passengers a choice of reaching Southampton.

In the latter part of the Nineteenth Century the London and South Western Railway Company (LSWR) was dominant in Hampshire but it was having great difficulty keeping the rival Great Western Railway Company (GWR) at bay. With GWR eyes firmly set in the direction of Southampton, the LSWR would counter attack by preparing schemes to Bristol, where local businessmen were as fed up with the domination of the GWR as its counterparts were in Southampton with the LSWR.

GWR saw its chance to reach Southampton by way of the independent Didcot, Newbury and Southampton Railway. The line opened from Didcot to Newbury in 1882. However the southern section was held up while various discussions took place with the Southampton Corporation Harbour Board, Chamber of Commerce and other local businessmen who all wanted the Didcot, Newbury and Southampton Railway (backed by

GWR) to extend its independent line from Whitchurch to Southampton without depending on the London and South Western Railway, saying that an alternative railway linking Southampton with the Midlands and the North would be a profitable enterprise.

Spurred into action by this the London and South Western Railway Company came up with its own scheme to link Southampton with the Midlands and the North. This included a new line just over seven miles long, to be built from the main London and South Western Railway Basingstoke-Salisbury line at Hurstbourne to a junction at Fullerton on the Andover and Redbridge Railway. An important part of the scheme was improving the Andover and Redbridge Railway by widening and straightening (including doubling the tracks). With Parliamentary approval the London and South Western Railway Company lost no time in getting work under way for its new line, impressively named Northern and Southern Junction Railway.

Constructing what seemed quite a short line from Hurstbourne to Fullerton was not an easy task, especially with heavy earthworks required between the main line near Hurstbourne and Longparish, also at Wherwell. Many of the navvies who constructed the line set up camp in the Longparish area of Harewood Forest at a spot which became known as 'Ten Huts', the name deriving from tin huts. At Wherwell there was one such camp in the area of the Mount. Unfortunately, as with nearly all heavy railway construction, several navvies were killed while carrying out the work.

The original station at Fullerton was opened as Fullerton Bridge, when the Andover to Redbridge line was opened in 1865, and was situated near the road between the river Anton and the river Test. In 1871 a new station, more centrally sited to the area, was built and when the new line to Hurstbourne was opened in 1885 received the rather grand title of Fullerton Junction, with four covered platforms, connected by a central canopied entranced ticket office. Although mostly of timber construction it had an attractive and pleasing appearance. The cost of constructing the line was £162,700.

On reaching Whitchurch the Didcot, Newbury and Southampton Railway Company spurned this sensible offer of a connection at Whitchurch and decided to push on with its own line which went underneath the London

Fullerton Junction Station showing the branch line canopied platform (reduced to single line). The cinder pathway, seen on the right of picture, was mostly used by travellers from Chilbolton.

Travelling tender first, a 'Jubilee' class 0-4-2 waits at Fullerton Junction with a single carriage for Wherwell, Longparish, Hurstbourne and Whitchurch. *(courtesy of Lens of Sutton)*

and South Western Line with a new station nearer the town. However, by the time it reached Winchester, having built a fine station at Chesil, the company was bankrupt.

Whitchurch Station, terminal of the Fullerton-Hurstbourne line, with a Fullerton train waiting in the siding. Note the spur at lower right of picture, provided for the proposed connection with the DNSR – then under construction and nearing Whitchurch.

Later it was forced to accept the crumbs the London and South Western Railway Company offered from its impregnable position. A junction was opened at Shawford on 1 October 1891 with no running powers – all trains had to be worked by the LSWR. Without the planned connection the Fullerton line became a backwater and reduced to single line operation in 1913.

On 1 June 1885 the new line from Hurstbourne to Fullerton opened for passenger traffic with Whitchurch as the northern terminal. The four daily departures from Whitchurch connected with trains from Waterloo. In order to generate more traffic, in 1890 train services were extended to Basingstoke, which became the departure point for the line, but in July 1924 reverted back to Whitchurch with just three daily trains up to closure in 1931.

The last through train to run over the line from Longparish and out on to the main line at Hurstbourne, before the junction was taken out of use, was a goods train containing all the stock from a farm at nearby Bransbury (owned by a Mr Hamilton) consisting of cattle, carts, horses and even the employees.

With passenger services withdrawn, the Hurstbourne junction taken out, the line was lifted in 1934 to a point approximately 200 yards north of Longparish Station, making this once through railway line into a branch line, worked 'up' from Fullerton. The station at Fullerton had already lost its title of Junction in July 1929, even though the line to Longparish stayed open for goods traffic until May 1956.

For several years in the 1920s a special train was used by the Priory to transport all the staff, including the grooms and horses, from Wherwell Station to Melton Mowbray in Leicestershire for hunting. They were away for a month. The horse boxes and two carriages were in the sidings several days before departure. I have memories of seeing them being loaded and again when the train passed within sight of our cottage and through the Mount cutting.

Although passenger traffic was very light, both Wherwell and Longparish Stations had a fair amount of goods traffic. Wherwell was kept busy by the nearby Chilbolton farmers who used the station as the main loading

Wherwell Station goods yard in the early 1900s. *(courtesy of Lens of Sutton)*

place for all their corn. They also despatched pressed hay for the Army and baled straw for use on strawberry beds. In addition there were coal supplies for the two coal merchants and building material for the builders (including father).

The last goods train hauled by a Drummond T9 class 4-4-0 locomotive departs for Longparish in 1956.
(The late Charles Eric Wardell collection – by courtesy of Jean Wardell-Davis)

From 1914 there was considerable activity at Longparish. Apart from the two coal yards, James Taylor Limited set up a sawmill at the rear of Longparish Station, it bordered on the edge of Harewood Forest and covered a wide area. A narrow gauge railway system was built there which also linked the sawmill with the station yard and by the early 1920s as many as 30 railway wagons per day were put to use for receiving and despatching timber products.

During the 1914-18 War the line was extensively used for troop movements.

In 1915 Messrs Kynock Limited of Birmingham erected a wood distillation factory adjoining Taylors Sawmill and requested the London and South Western Railway Company to provide siding accommodation. It was built and in use the following year. Over 100 people were employed at the Kynock factory and a special daily train ran between Whitchurch and Longparish to convey many of them. The weekly output of products from the factory (ranging from charcoal to wood oil) was about 1,000 tons and nearly all of it was transported by rail.

Hundreds of trees were felled in Harewood Forest, which were predominantly oak, and hauled by heavy horses with drag chains to the factory. Thomas Baverstock, the Chilbolton village blacksmith, regularly rode his bicycle, or walked, to the factory to shoe the horses. Such was the demand for timber that trees were also felled in Savernake Forest and transported by rail to Longparish Station.

In 1917 the Government took over the plant and worked it until July 1919 when production apparently ceased.

Later the site was acquired by Messrs Kennedy and Kempe Limited and known as Harewood Forest Works. With a new factory construction it was used for engineering purposes. The company was set up by two retired Army officers from the Great War (Colonel Kennedy and Captain Kempe) who had both served with the Royal Tank Corp. They were minded of single purpose and foresight to establish their own business after the War, specifically to manufacture wheelband tracks.

Mr E A Dennison, formerly with Taskers Engineering Works at Anna Valley, joined the company and later became the Managing Director. Mr Dennison lived at Clatford and daily travelled by train to Longparish Station. In later years he was chauffeur driven by Bert Cole of Longparish.

Appointed Contractors to the Ministry of Supply at the outbreak of the Second Great War, manufacturing output from the works increased rapidly to include tracks for six-wheeled lorries, earth anchors (used for tethering barrage balloons), spare wheel carriers, strakes for farm tractors, grain drying machines and grain storage plant. Machining the fabricated and welded steel work was also undertaken. As with Kynocks, nearly all of it was transported by rail, some as far away as Scotland. The narrow gauge railway system there was put to good use and also linked the company to the station sidings.

Well over 100 people were employed at Kennedy and Kempe, including some from Wherwell and Chilbolton. From Chilbolton, Henry Poore was a loyal and long serving employee. He joined the company when he left school in 1942 and, apart from his two years National Service in the Army, completed 39 years' service. Henry was first put to work cutting lengths of steel and later progressed to become a skilled welder. His first pay packet was 19 shillings and 3 pence. In 1942 Henry and his brothers and sisters were living with their grandparents, Mr and Mrs Thomas Baverstock, at their Horseshoe Cottage home in Chilbolton. His father was serving at sea with the Royal Navy during the Second Great War. Henry and his wife now live in Andover and I regularly keep in touch with them.

Also working there was Lou Harding from Wherwell, a skilled metal lathe turner. After Lou retired he produced some fine metal scale models using his own lathe, which I was privileged to see. In my view his masterpiece was a working scale model of a Garrett Steam Wagon, some three feet in length. Sadly Lou is no longer with us.

During the Second Great War the line reached its peak when it handled a tremendous amount of military traffic, mainly from an RAF Maintenance Unit which was set up at Longparish as an ammunition storage depot in October 1942. The RAF needed a stretch of woodland, not too close to a town, rail served and about 25 miles inland, and Harewood Forest met

Looking north at Longparish Station showing the concrete area where ammunition was loaded and unloaded during World War II. *(courtesy of Lens of Sutton)*

this requirement. War-time alterations were made to the sidings and a large concrete area was laid to facilitate loading and unloading. A new loop siding was added, built on the site of the 'up' side of the original double track, which was lifted in 1913.

The ammunition stored by the RAF in Harewood Forest was mainly bombs and bullets, which were kept in small huts, linked to the railway siding by concrete roads, which extended to the Wherwell-Andover road between Windwhistle and the White House. The ammunition was unloaded from the trains with the help of mobile cranes and then driven to the huts by RAF personnel using small tractors and trailers. By the end of 1943 nearly 600 wagons of blockbuster bombs arrived by rail each month and by June 1944 it was rumoured that as many as 6,000 wagon loads of bombs and bullets were stored in the forest.

At Fullerton additional sidings were put in to cope with the huge volume of traffic, two of which connected with the branch line and extended the full length of the approach road to the station, with a sentry box at the entrance. A further new siding at the north end of the station connected the main Andover to Redbridge line with the branch, which necessitated the cutting back of the length of the 'up' branch platform, and from the main line a siding was laid behind the 'up' platform.

Looking north at Longparish Station with a Drummond T9 under the loading gantry.
(courtesy of Lens of Sutton)

For another reason, a length of track was relaid at the face of the down line branch platform and beyond (which was lifted in 1913) to accommodate carriages used by office workers after the heavy bombing at Southampton Station. Wherwell Station was reduced to just one siding, which extended to the full length of the yard. The buffer stop was buttressed with concrete. For particular locomotives the steep gradient through the Mount cutting was just too much for a slow (hardly moving) heavy train, for it would come to a halt. It then reversed back to Wherwell Station siding for part of the train to be uncoupled – the easy part!

After the War was over and troops returned home for demobilisation, the nearby Barton Stacey Camp was used to house the Americans and many troop trains travelled up the line to Longparish.

At about the same time the ammunition store in Harewood Forest was increased when other similar units, which were being closed down elsewhere, sent their stocks to the forest for disposal. Some of the ammunition was sold and transported abroad, while the job of clearing up and transporting for disposal took some years, and it was not until the early 1950s that the task was considered to be over.

Constructed from a metal die-cast kit,
my impressive scale model of a Drummond 'T9' class 4-4-0 locomotive in LSWR livery.

The final goods service over the line was on 28 May 1956. After this date the line was used for the storage of condemned wagons and vans (which blighted the view from our cottage), and extended to the buffer stop beyond Longparish Station. It was also used for testing the Southern Region's new diesel multiple units before they went into service in the area with an hourly service from Andover to Portsmouth, but initially it was worked with steam trains. Finally, some condemned electric stock was stored on the branch at Fullerton.

In the 1920s the Jubilee class locomotive 0-4-2 worked the line. Without a turntable it ran tender-first in one direction. The train consisted of one coach and a six-wheeled parcel-brake van. Goods trains were mostly worked with a Drummond T9 4-4-0 locomotive.

For economy purposes, in March 1928 a four-wheeled Drewry Petrol Railcar was tried on the line. It proved to be unsuccessful, due in part to the steep gradients encountered, and was withdrawn. (I often watched its slow progress as it laboured through the Mount cutting – one of the steepest gradients on the line.) Unusual in appearance was the prominence of its 'lorry style' radiator seen in front of the bodywork.

The Drewry Petrol Railcar which was used on the line.
(The late Dr I C Allen, courtesy of Peter A Harding)

The line was immaculately kept, paths and verges on both sides were kept free of weeds and falling chalk from the deep cuttings. The linesman responsible for this lived in one of the railway cottages at Longparish. He often used a four-wheeled trolley on the line. Selected parts of the verge area were used as vegetable gardens. One such place was by the lower part of the Mount – sweet peas were also grown, a favourite then. The linesmen had this privilege. They also had a hut nearby – known as a plate-layer's hut. Wild strawberries also grew on the lower Mount bank.

At Dublin Farm a brick formed land drainage tunnel some 50 feet in length and 2 feet in diameter ran underneath the embankment. It was a challenge for the boys to crawl through it – even me, but only in summertime. We all wore short trousers then but came to no harm, despite the mud and stones.

Generally speaking we did not trespass on the line - but for me it was a short cut to home, although I was fond of walking up the line to Dublin and back by road. It was a pleasant Sunday afternoon walk.

Railway bridge with superb arched brickwork at Dublin Farm, known as first arch.
A second arch beyond it was demolished.

The history of the line would not be complete without mentioning that in 1927 Piccadilly Pictures filmed several scenes for the cinema version of Arnold Ridley's play 'The Ghost Train'. Longparish Station was mainly featured for the scenes shot on 11, 12 and 13 April which included the famous mail-bag robbery. For one scene a realistic brick wall, mostly constructed of cardboard, was erected across the line a short distance below the down platform. It was night-time, a howling gale and torrential rain, cold and shivering passengers patiently awaiting their train, when suddenly out of the darkness a sustained piercing whistle – the ghost train thundered through the station and disappeared through the brick wall with a devastating effect. Passengers were horror stricken and frightened – no doubt Arnold Ridley was on hand to comfort and console them! My brother was there to see some of the action, but for me it was bedtime. The film was shown later in the year at the Palace Theatre, Andover and billed as a film of local interest. Arnold Ridley was well known to us in later years as Private Godfrey in the television comedy series 'Dad's Army'.

Walking across Above Town on one of my favourite Sunday afternoon walks, which provided a panoramic view of the station yard below, I was fortunate to see a special train pass through carrying equipment for the action. In one wagon an aeroplane engine with propeller, mounted in a timber framed crate, was used to provide the hurricane force gale. A fire engine provided the torrential rain.

I always enjoyed travelling by train, my first was just a penny fare from Fullerton Junction to Wherwell, a three minute journey. I had been playing with a friend at Cottonworth Farm House on a Saturday afternoon. After tea his mother took me to the station, paid my fare and put me on the 6.10 pm train, saying "get out when the train stops".

During school holidays in the late 1920s and early 1930s, together with my brother and sister, mother would take us to Southsea by train for our summer holidays, which was usually for two weeks. Exciting for me was the train journey, so much to see on the way with the hustle and bustle at each station. Especially to watch the shunter's pole coupling and uncoupling goods trucks in the sidings, then the sharp clanging sound as they buffered up – not seen or heard now. The signal box was another attraction, with an eye on the signals as the levers were pulled. Then the swishing up and down of the telegraph wires on the journey. (So enthused was I that it was during this period that I formed the Wherwell Hornby Railway Club.)

Built to main line standard – impressive Wherwell Station 15-levers signal-box with signalman.
(courtesy of Lens of Sutton)

Southsea was such a delightful place then for a holiday – I looked forward to it every year, saving up my hard-earned pennies week by week to spend in the delightful toy shops there. For me South Parade Pier was so attractive, the two uniformed attendants at the Pier entrance were kept busy at the turn-stiles with a loud click, click, click as each visitor passed through. The Pier toll was 2d. At the Pier head a military band entertained us daily. Fascinating for me was to watch the paddle steamers tie up and depart from the Pier head landing stage, then the thrill to see the paddle wheels whipping up the water to a crescendo as they departed. But more exciting was to enjoy excursion trips to the Isle of Wight and to Southampton Docks for inspection of huge liners, which then were Aquitania, Olympic, Majestic and Empress of Australia. The Southern Railway's impressive

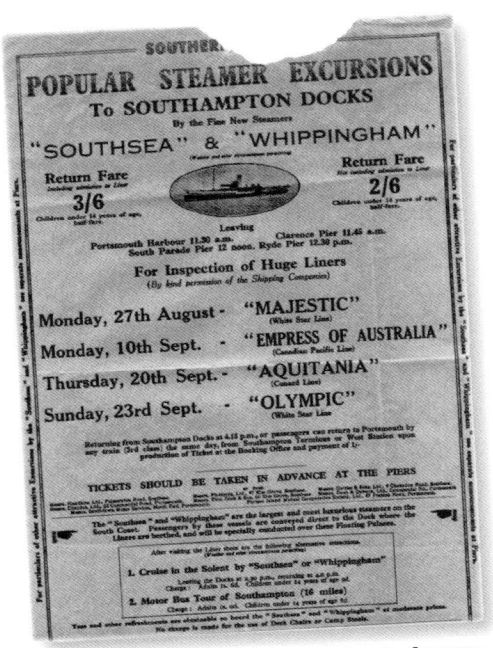

Southern Railway advertisement for Popular Steamer Excursions from Southsea. *(courtesy of Ken Braxton)*

and largest new paddle steamers, *Southsea* and *Whippingham*, both with a carrying capacity of 1,200 passengers, were used for these popular trips to the Southern Railway owned Southampton Docks. How proud I was to be a passenger on them. The fare was 2/6d for adults and half-price for children. Displayed on the sea front were the names of liners passing each day.

Another delight was to visit Portsmouth Dockyard during Navy Week, which was a week of activities and events. It was so exciting to go on board huge battleships, two I remember were *HMS Hood* and *HMS Rodney*. Then there was the aircraft carrier *HMS Courageous*. I was truly amazed with the cramped conditions as we passed through the narrow passageways in a submarine. A guided tour on-board Nelson's *HMS Victory* was an unforgettable delight. On leaving the ship mother bought a souvenir piece of oak from the ship's ongoing restoration work.

Another fascination for me was the sight and sound of the tramway system, and to enjoy tram rides. Most were open fronted at both ends – no need then to turn the tram around, as with a bus. The longitudinal wooden seats with a shallow well – perhaps to prevent passengers sliding off with the gentle swaying motion of the tram gave a comfortable ride! I enjoyed watching the driver, in a standing position at the controls. During wet weather the driver wore a cape – much the same as policemen did. The wording displayed on the Portsmouth Corporation crest, which adorned both sides of the trams 'Heaven's Light our Guide' was, I thought, divinely inspired and most appropriate.

We also used Wherwell Station for our Easter holidays to Hartley Wintney, changing at Whitchurch and Basingstoke and alighting at Winchfield. We stayed with an aunt, where I particularly remember a wind-up gramophone with a large horn attached to the sound-box. A popular record of the day was 'Bye bye Blackbird'. It was there that I first learned to ride my cousin's bicycle. On the return journey, before leaving Whitchurch for Wherwell, in inclement weather the guard would switch on the carriage lights by a lever at the rear of the carriage. This was much to 'lighten our darkness' as we passed through the deep cuttings towards Longparish.

How fortunate we were then to be able to catch a train from the village station and what an impressive building it was with a smart canopied entrance, adorned with attractive balustrade and a unique arched dormer window above in the roof space, which was boarded. Adjoining the spacious booking hall was a comfortable waiting room, and on the platform a machine dispensing Nestlé chocolate bars. It could boast a private road with an entrance at both ends. Lattice style fencing adorned the stationmaster's garden and the two railway cottages. The station was an impressive feature of the village scene. I often used the station road in my walks.

The stationmaster's house adjoined the station, his name was Allen. I often would find him there when I was sent to the station by father to collect parcels, which sometimes would be in the parcel shed sited on the down platform. A pen and ink, with relief nib, was used to sign the parcel receipt book – always kept on a shelf under the booking office window.

A panoramic view looking down on Wherwell Station area with the double track line and goods yard siding soon after the line opened. The lower end of the approach road can also be seen. *(courtesy of Lens of Sutton)*

Oil lamps, then the norm, were used for lighting, apart from the station and platform; there were three column lamps along station road. The oil shed was sited at the lower end of the former 'up' platform. The station's water supply was hand pumped from a pump shed on the 'down' platform.

No less than 16 bridges formed part of the line, mostly of brick arched construction, those built for access for farm land were known as occupation bridges. The skew bridge near Apsley Farm, the third from Hurstbourne Junction, was built with twin brick arches for the double track and quite impressive. The two iron road bridges at Wherwell and Cottonworth were regularly cleaned and repainted and the verges kept free of weeds.

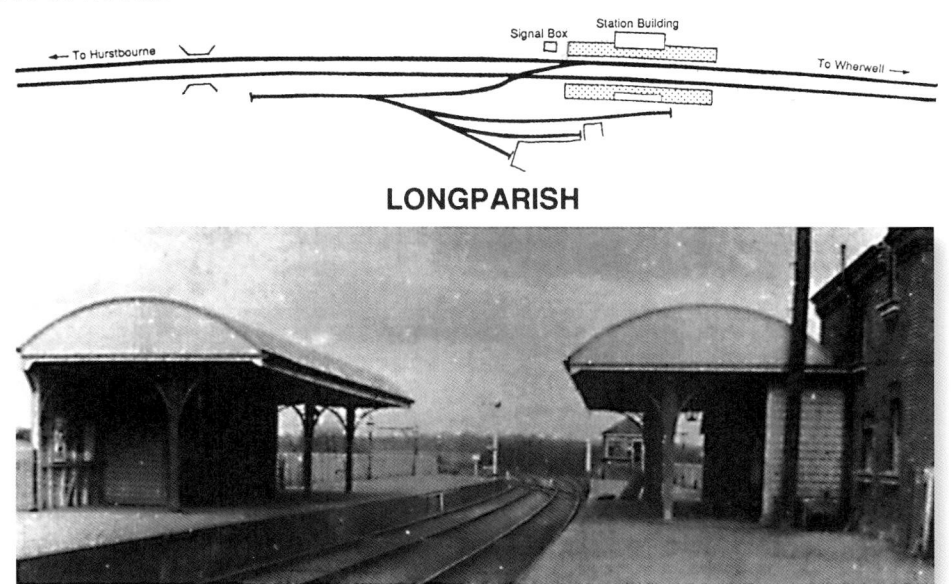

LONGPARISH

Longparish Station looking north towards Hurstbourne. The station buildings were similar in design and construction to Wherwell. The goods yard sidings were approached from the A303.
(N J Lambourne Collection, courtesy of Peter A Harding)

In charge of the permanent way the lengthsman daily walked the track between Fullerton and Stockbridge to carry out a safety check of the line for possible damage, subsidence or obstruction, as sometimes caused by fallen tree branches, before the first daily train passed over it. Usually over his shoulder he carried a long handled hammer used for securing the wooden wedge blocks in the iron rail chairs. Constant vibration with each passing train caused them to loosen and dislodge. He lived in the railway cottages at Fullerton Station with his fellow employees, the signalman and porter.

Such was my enthusiasm for train travel that when I started work in the early thirties my one week's holiday was a seven day runabout ticket for unlimited travel from Fullerton to Southampton and Portsmouth, which included Salisbury; all of this for seven shillings and sixpence. The three coach trains were non-corridor stock and of wood construction. On the last train from Southampton (9.00 pm) the guard would extinguish the platform lights at each station after leaving Romsey.

An extract from the Andover Advertiser 1959 read: "The British Transport Commission has agreed to sell Wherwell railway station, which includes the station house and two other cottages, to Andover Rural District Council for £1,875. Announcing this fact at Friday's monthly meeting of the council the Chairman, Mr J D Threadgill, said that it was hoped that possession would be made available early in 1959. In the meantime, he said the council will seek permission to let the station house, pending the completion of purchase, in order to prevent deterioration and damage to the building as at present it was empty. He also said that the council representatives had asked the railway authority when the accumulation of trucks on the line running through the station would be moved. At present there are several hundred condemned trucks standing idle on the line from Fullerton Junction through Wherwell to Longparish. The council had been assured that the trucks would be moved by the end of the year, said Mr Threadgill."

Condemned trucks on the line before lifting.

Wendy on the track at the southern end of Wherwell Station at the time of lifting.

Railway cutting approaching Wherwell Station with Hillside Cottages depicted on the right beyond the bridge. *(courtesy of Lens of Sutton)*

The end of Queen Victoria's allegedly favourite railway line – demolition scene of Wherwell Station 1959. *(The late Charles Eric Wardell – by courtesy of Jean Wardell-Davis)*

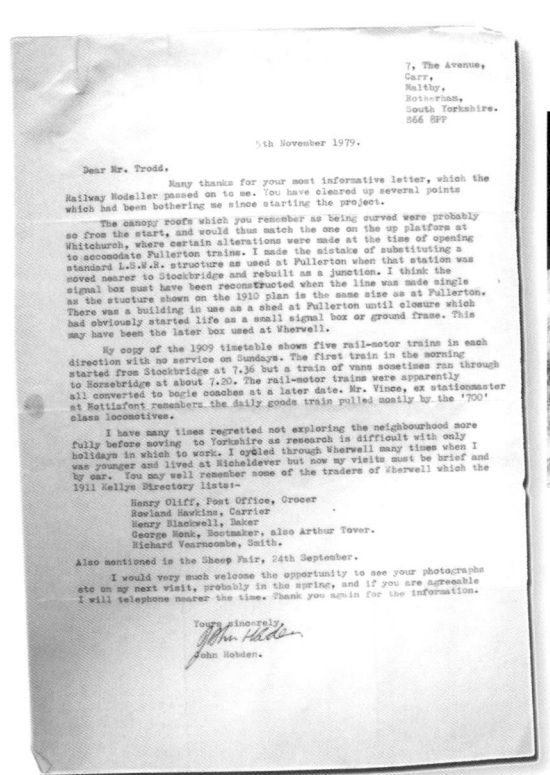

The best of what remains of John Hobden's construction of Wherwell station – the two bridges and Hillside Cottages.

John Hobden's reply to my letter following his 'Wherwell Station' article in the Railway Modeller Magazine, October 1979.

The Wherwell Car (1920-21)

The following advertisement appeared in the Light Car and Cyclecar publication dated 30 October 1920: 'Messrs Thompson and Son, Wherwell, near Andover, Hampshire, are putting upon the market an extremely simple proposition which is to be known as the 'Wherwell'.

The 'Wherwell' has a wheelbase of 7 feet 6 inches and a track of 3 feet 10 inches, whilst its weight, unladen, is 4.5 hundredweight. Without accessories the price of the machine is £130. Delivery can be given, to order only within one month from the date it is placed.

The car was powered by a Coventry Victor air-cooled engine – a horizontal twin developing 7-horse power. 'Wherwell' was a two-seater sports, driven by a chain/belt to the back axle, and had pneumatic tyres. There was no differential on the model. It had four forward gears and a fixed sloping bonnet; petrol was poured through the bonnet cap.

Mr Thompson, who had retired after being chauffeur to Miss Beddington at Longstock Park, moved to Wherwell and lived with his son in one of the new Fair Piece semi-detached houses. He rented a shed in Mr Spratt's yard in Fullerton Road, and it was there with his son that three cars were constructed. There was diversification along the way, including a belt drive to one model and various changes to the body style. There was no unification in design. It is more than likely they were kept busy with continuous modifications, which meant that all the time the costs were mounting. The very basic type of shed they had to work in, especially during the winter with little light or heat, did not help.

One of the cars was owned by David Young of Westover Farm, Lower Clatford. It is said that David, who was used to handling horses, tried the 'Wherwell' out in a field and temporarily forgetting the 'new fangled' method of stopping this then novel form of transport, went hurtling and bouncing along over the grass, clutching grimly at the wheel and yelling '"whoa" at the top of his voice! Incredibly, he would hitch his 'Wherwell' to a horse – the transmission was not too satisfactory over rough ground – and then go ambling over the fields learning to steer.

His bailiff used to drive the car; he seemed impressed with it and often drove it as far as Winchester and Salisbury, but unfortunately not having mastered the art of negotiating the 'Wherwell' he turned it over in a ditch.

Later, Robert Burnfield of Little Ann Farm (David Young was his uncle) used the car and ran it until about 1927. He said that it was quite capable of 40 to 50 miles per hour on the straight, and was lively and quite reliable. Thompson and Son later advertised it as capable of climbing Hurstbourne Hill in second gear whilst carrying two people.

The clutch and gear system, according to Robert Burnfield, worked on a system almost like placing two dinner plates together at an angle of 90 degrees with fibre friction contacts, four speeds on one side and one reverse on the other. There was a hole in the middle of one plate – which allowed the rim of the other plate to spin at the centre without contacting, consequently producing neutral.

The other two 'Wherwells' were sold to William (Bill) Spratt and a baker in Romsey.

Mr Thompson was wise in his decision not to continue with the 'Wherwell', for hot on his heels was Herbert Austin with advanced plans for his Austin Seven. The Seven went into production in 1922 and was exhibited at

Olympia in the same year. Priced at £225, it was an immediate success. The construction was more conventional with a four-cylinder engine and prop shaft drive from the gearbox to a rear axle with differential.

At least the 'Wherwell' had four wheels; most of the early small cars were three-wheelers – such as the well-known BSA and Morgan – and were fitted with the same type of engine.

The innovative 'Wherwell' car built in 1921 at Wherwell.

Wherwell itself was rich in talent and enterprise in those early days; early motor transport played a part in it but sadly, as with the railway, it did not survive. Wherwell therefore has a claim of having been one of the centres of initial private endeavour from which the motor industry developed!

Hampshire County Council Museums Service approached me for a story of the 'Wherwell' car and followed this with a visit from a member of staff.

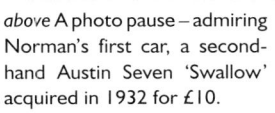

above A photo pause – admiring Norman's first car, a second-hand Austin Seven 'Swallow' acquired in 1932 for £10.

My transport:
(left to right, top to bottom)

Raleigh motorcycle CG 7658 purchased in 1936 for £30.00

AJS motorcycle GJO 998 purchased in 1939 for £40.00

Austin Seven De-luxe Saloon CG 6677 purchased in 1942 for £42.10s.0d.

Austin Seven 'Ruby' BLO 548 purchased in 1944 for £50.00

Austin Ten De-luxe Saloon AYH 428 purchased in 1956 as an ex part exchange for £30.00

Chapter 9

Religious and Other Groups

The Iron Room

The Iron Room – the village hall – was erected through the kindness and at the expense of Lady Agneta Montague of the Priory.

The timber-framed building was clad with galvanised iron – hence the name Iron Room. The interior was lined with tongued and grooved matchboard, stained and varnished. There was no ceiling but the roof was boarded. The vortex board fixed to the apex extended the whole length of the roof with ventilation holes at regular intervals.

The front porch was very small and only the width of the door; there was a ventilator window above.

There was very little light to brighten it, windows were only fitted to the west side. The east side was bare, except for a picture of a seaplane. Two anti-rooms were provided, one either side of the hall. On the left was a kitchen with a small kitchen range, accessed from the stage. On the right it was a cloakroom with steps provided to access the stage from the floor of the hall. Both rooms also had an exterior door for access from the pathways either side of the hall.

The height of the stage was about two feet. Velvet curtains ringed to a steel pole extended to the full width which was about 18 feet. The pole was centrally held in place with a steel rod fixed to the roof apex.

Heating was by an open fire, it was near the stage on the west side (probably to keep this area warmer). It was enclosed with a substantial fireguard. Lighting was by oil lamps – two either side. For the pianist the piano was fitted with two swivelling brass mounted candle holders.

The Iron Room was a popular venue for meetings, parties, dramas, whist drives, the Women's Institute and much more. Mother was a member of the Wherwell Players. She enjoyed acting and could use her musical gifts at the piano. Occasionally a travelling show would visit to entertain us. One of the songs I remember went:

> *On the road, on the road,*
> *On the road to anywhere,*
> *Where the milestones seem to say …*

The Iron Room served Wherwell for over 70 years. It was replaced in 1957 with a modern hall, again by a benefactor of Wherwell Priory, Mrs Jenkins in memory of her husband, Colonel A E Jenkins.

The Abstinence Union

This was founded in 1855 as a society for promoting temperance principles among the young by advocating self-control to abstain from the consumption of alcoholic liquor.

Up until the 1890s meetings were held fortnightly in the Iron Room by the kind permission of Lady Agneta Montague, a passionate supporter of the Union. Mr J Rodaway, a staunch Methodist supporter and preacher, lived in the cottage opposite the Iron Room and presided over one such meeting. Lady Agneta also attended on one occasion. It was in 1883/84 when the railway was being constructed that drunkenness was a problem in the village.

When just a girl mother regularly attended and would use her musical talent at the piano. She was taught to play by her aunt, who lived in Ivy Cottage, just a few yards from the Iron Room.

For us in the 1920s the Union was known as the Band of Hope. Meetings were then held monthly and, as children, we were very much a lively part of the proceedings. We all loved to get on stage with our act, such as recitations, monologues, songs or playing an instrument.

Mrs Prangley (a Sunday school teacher) was also a popular addition as she played her mandolin, with her daughter Christine at the piano, for singing temperance songs. For this we had a special songbook. Generally we would sing two songs, but if time allowed it was three. We were usually in full voice, especially with the chorus, one of which I remember went:

> *Dare, dare, dare to be right,*
> *Dare, dare, dare to be true …*

A visiting speaker would address the meeting expounding the benefits of total abstinence, of self-control and discipline to refrain from strong drink. Of course we were always asked to sign the pledge. The meetings would close with the Doxology – Praise God from whom all Blessings flow. They were happy cheerful meetings, always well supported and always enjoyed. Some of us had to sit on forms as there were not enough chairs.

The Women's Institute and 'Living Whist'

Mother was a founding member of the Wherwell Women's Institute. I still have her membership badge.

The 'Living Whist' event was the Women's Institute at its best with members from both Wherwell and Chilbolton forming much of the pack, including my mother and sister – children were also allowed.

All those who participated became 'living' playing cards and dressed in costumes to represent each suit of cards. Mother was dressed as the Ace of Diamonds and my sister was one of the Hearts' suit. The members made the costumes at their own expense – nearly all had a sewing machine in those days. I remember my mother had a Fritzer and Rossman, I always enjoyed turning the handle for her.

'Living Whist' – a fine pack of Chilbolton and Wherwell residents display their charm.
Back row, third from left is mother; third row, second from left is Vera.

The game was played by 56 players – 52 to form the pack – thirteen teams of four players. It was played at Broxton Court, Chilbolton in the thirties and previously it was at Down End. It was extremely interesting to watch and quite colourful.

Wherwell Choral Society

The choir took part in the annual Winchester Musical Festival Banner at the Guildhall, Winchester.

In 1928 some 65 choirs competed. Points were awarded for sight-reading, test choruses, two- and three-part songs and a madrigal. Wherwell members returned home with a banner.

Successful Wherwell Choral Society proudly display the Winchester Musical Festival Banner at the Vicarage (with Mr Tovey and family members).

Wherwell had an abundance of musical talent in the 1920s, and Chilbolton too. My music teacher was from Chilbolton, her father was a local farmer (her brother Norman was a pupil at Andover Grammar School with my brother). George Duckett, also from Chilbolton, was headteacher at Chilbolton Village School, he was also an accomplished organist and played at Chilbolton Church and later at Wherwell Church. Christine Prangley and Doris Hayes both played the organ at Wherwell Church, as did mother on occasions. In 1922 Stainer's Crucifixion was sung on Good Friday in the church. I still have mother's music from this and it is more than likely that George Duckett was the organist.

The Early Methodist Movement and Wherwell Wesleyan Methodist Chapel

The history of Wherwell Wesleyan Methodist Chapel is a tale of power, bribery and intrigue.

One of the key players in the drama was James Tovey the elder – an early Wesleyan stalwart. He was a young man when he came to Wherwell in or about the year 1817. He was a true and warm-hearted person who opened his house for prayer meetings.

Such was the response that two cottages were used as a chapel. These were situated in the chalk pit at Greenwich, opposite Dublin Farm. They were occupied by John Dugey, a carpenter, and Elizabeth Inglefield, a widow. Certificates for worship were obtained by the Superintendent Minister of the Winchester Wesleyan circuit and the two homes became the first Wesleyan Methodist Chapel at Wherwell. The lower rooms were made into one, with part of the upper floor removed and part left in position to provide a gallery. Membership increased yearly and reached 30.

By 1845 it was resolved to build a chapel. This was not easy as the local landowners were not likely to provide a site, but there was a way and they did not have to wait long. The Priory did not own all the land. James Tovey and Charles Batt, the blacksmith, heard that three cottages in the Court, owned by a lady in Basingstoke, were for sale. Without mentioning their purpose to anyone they went to Basingstoke, taking with them enough money to pay the deposit on a possible purchase of the properties. Their journey was worthwhile as they were successful. Divinely inspired Charles Batt bought the cottages for the Wherwell Wesleyans at some personal inconvenience. It was wonderful - a prime prominent central site for the new Wesleyan Methodist Chapel in the heart of the village, a truly remarkable achievement.

At that time the Priory and the established church were opposed to any extension of Methodism in Wherwell. It was regarded as undesirable and unwanted, with a divisive influence for it also strongly supported the Abstinence Union in strict temperance. Even in my younger days people living in tied cottages, and working for the Priory Estate, were expected to attend church. It was the independent part of the village that supported and aligned with the Methodists.

In the meantime steps had to be taken to circumvent the expected opposition. The Methodists pulled down and removed the old chalk pit chapel which allowed the parishioners to believe that a new chapel would be built on that site. They even dug trenches for a foundation and so the smoke-screen continued until the conveyance was completed and the new site made secure.

When it became known that the Wesleyan Methodists had obtained a new site for the chapel, and in the centre of the village, there was a great stir and the opposing powers explored every possible means to wrest possession from Charles Batt. He was offered double the price he had paid for the purchase and, when bribery failed, the opposition resorted to threats, but it was in vain. James Tovey and his friends paid Charles Batt £100 for the two cottages near the street, and the other he sold in order to repay a mortgage he had taken up.

The foundation stones of the new chapel were laid in the spring of 1846. The Chairman of the District conducted the Service of Dedication. The first hymn was aptly chosen, it was 'Except the Lord conduct the plan, the best concerted schemes are vain and never can succeed'.

A trust was formed to hold the property for the purposes of the Wesleyan Methodist connection. The Memoranda of Trustees consisted of:
George Alexander of Wherwell – market gardener
James Dance of Longparish – miller
John Hawkins of Houghton – grinder
William Hillier of Andover – hairdresser
Henry Mitchener of Wherwell – labourer
Thomas Neil of Wallop – baker
Robert Smith of Wherwell – waterman
William Spreadbury of Longparish – miller
James Tovey of Wherwell – cordwainer
James Tovey the younger of Wherwell – cordwainer
George Whitcher of Broughton – grocer
John Withers of Longparish – yeoman.

On 31 October 1846 the Chapel was licensed for worship, the circuit minister conducted the opening service. The congregation sang Isaac Watts call to worship:

Lord of the worlds above
How pleasant and how fair
The dwellings of Thy love
Thine earthly temples are
To thine abode
My heart aspires
With warm desires
To meet my God.

It was an inspired choice, for no words more fittingly described their gratitude and aspiration, aided by the words from Psalm 84 'They go from strength to strength'. It was a memorable service; the experience of divine power was felt by all. Those joyful Methodists cherished the memories of it and passed on the story of that happy day to their children.

But their joy was soon clouded as the opposition, although frustrated, remained powerful. They could not prevent the Methodists from building a house of worship but they could make life difficult for the builders of the chapel, and this they proceeded to do. James Tovey and his family received notice to quit their Priory cottage and, as no other accommodation could be found in the village, they had to find a new home in Longparish. Charles Batt was the Priory blacksmith; he too was dismissed and as he could not find a home or employment in the village he emigrated to Canada. His removal seemed likely to inflict an irreparable loss upon the society, for he was a man of spiritual power. Few men exceeded his knowledge of the word of God, and he possessed profound insight into its message and power in preaching it.

It is sad to think that the Priory in those days was so displeased with the stalwarts of the Methodist cause and the building of their new chapel. Some of the Priory servants attended the services and although their employers were angry and called upon them to choose either to cease going to chapel or to leave their service, they chose the latter, which was of course a great sacrifice. They did not suffer in vain.

When these two pillars of the society left the village their enemies prophesised that local Methodism would die. They were mistaken. The great Head of the Church overruled persecution for the advancement of His work. James Tovey, the younger, remained and was distinguished for his beautiful singing and his able leadership of the choir and orchestra. As class leader, local preacher and society steward he became the spiritual leader.

Prayer meetings and class meetings were well attended. James Tovey was organist for 50 years, Sunday school superintendent and also my Sunday school teacher. His life was devoted to the work of his master in 'This temple of His Grace', and also to Wherwell. He was also a fine cricketer and loved his bat, he played for Wherwell winning the cup. I remember his bat was in our cottage after his passing, as was his organ. James Tovey possessed a magnetic personality, richly endowed with spiritual and musical gifts. He passed away in 1928.

It can be said that the society influenced the entire neighbourhood. People both young and old came from Chilbolton, Newton Stacey, Barton Stacey and Fullerton, and from other places more distant for the sincere Christian fellowship and spiritual uplifting.

Long Service Certificate presented to James Arthur Tovey in recognition of 40 years' service with the Wherwell Sunday School.

In the second Memoranda of Trustees appointed in March 1887 the impressive team comprised:
    Josiah Broundon of Andover – builder
    Williams Arthur Gillingham of Andover – grocer's assistant
    Thomas Hobbs the elder of Hurstbourne Priors – clerk of works
    William Thomas Hobbs the younger of Hurstbourne Priors – carpenter
    Charles Frank Jones of Whitchurch – jeweller
    Arthur Lambourne of Andover – clerk
    James Reynolds of Longparish – gardener
    John Thomas Rodaway of Wherwell – relieving officer
    James Arthur Tovey the younger of Wherwell – cordwainer

William Tovey of Longparish – cordwainer
Frederick William Turley of Wherwell – gardener.

John Rodaway lived in the thatched cottage opposite the village hall. He was another outstanding personality and gave 25 years' service to the chapel, not only as a most faithful local preacher but also as a Sunday school teacher. He and James Tovey took the first class of boys and girls with two other teachers for the second class. At that time the scholars numbered between 50 and 60; roughly about the same as in my time.

The chapel anniversary was always a very popular festival. The public meeting in the week was always followed by a coffee supper – a popular event in those days. There were always generous and willing helpers in the village.

In 1896 the chapel anniversary suffered a rare misfortune caused by a wet Sunday. The preacher from Tytherley, a village some 10 miles away, failed to arrive. He had set out from his home by cycle but, becoming drenched by the heavy rain, returned home. The teachers managed the morning service and in the afternoon Mr Harry Willshire borrowed Mr Spratt's cycle, rode into Andover and prevailed on Alderman William McLoughlin to take the evening service, which he did. He preached from the words "I beg your pardon, I am very sorry". The chapel was built with a gallery and on that occasion there were 47 seated. The total congregation was well over 100, a remarkable figure.

Alderman McLoughlin, a coal merchant, was a gifted man. He was an attractive and persuasive orator, and a driving force behind any good cause. He became Mayor of Andover in 1903. Harry Willshire was then a young man from a Wherwell family who later left the village. In 1906 he became Secretary of the Brotherhood Movement and was also connected with Christian Endeavour. His name was later added to the Andover Wesleyan Circuit Plan of Local Preachers. I can remember him taking services at Wherwell.

Not even the worst weather would prevent John Rodaway from keeping his preaching appointments for the Andover Wesleyan Methodist circuit. In the winter he often walked eight miles to Wallop over the downs in driving rain or snow. He and Mrs Rodaway extended hospitality to others in their home and in the summer it was their pleasure to regale their guests with strawberries from their garden.

In later years it was Harry Young and his family who lived there; he too was a stalwart and was appointed joint superintendent with James Tovey. He loved Charles Wesley's hymns. Such was his expression of spiritual feeling that he would raise and lower his hymn book as if in tune with the music. He was a farmer, haulier and dairyman. His son Fred carried on the business after him.

Another Wherwell man was George Lawrence – a man of grace and power – and a gifted preacher in the late 1880s. Though totally blind he walked the circuit unaided to keep his appointments. His knowledge of the scriptures and of the Methodist hymn book was wide and accurate. Rarely did he use his Braille Bible in public, but studied it at home. A friend gave him a clock, which he carried in his pocket and read the time on its face with his fingers. The uninitiated wondered how the blind man knew the time so well. He was an outstanding character. We must remember in those days that Sunday must have offered a welcome break from the daily toil. There was a great respect for Sunday – it truly was a day of rest.

I often wonder how Charles Batt and James Tovey got to Basingstoke. The railway to Andover did not open until 1854, so then it must have been by foot or possibly horseback. One must admire their commitment and endeavour.

During my boyhood there were two local preachers living in the village: Tom Spratt, relieving officer *(an official appointed to supervise the relief of the parish poor)*, and George Prangley, a builder. Mrs Prangley also became a Sunday school teacher.

Mother maintained the great Tovey tradition of organ playing after James Tovey's death in 1928 and continued playing for 47 years.

Brass tablet erected in Wherwell Wesleyan Methodist Chapel in memory of James Arthur Tovey, 1928.

Wherwell Wesleyan Methodist ladies at the pathway to the vestry – each with a posy of flowers and pictured leaving the chapel after Sunday worship.

The history of the chapel was gloriously mixed with devotion, persecution and success. Local preachers came to preach from all over the circuit which included Leckford, Stockbridge, Houghton, Nether Wallop, Abbotts Ann, Thruxton, Weyhill, Collingbourne, St Mary Bourne, Whitchurch, Overton and Andover. Some walked, some cycled – very few had the luxury of a car. Mother could remember one preacher arriving on horseback. Such was their zeal that very few failed to keep their appointments, even in winter.

In the early days oil stoves were used for heating and hanging oil lamps for lighting, with two mounted oil lamps either side of the pulpit. A central heating system was installed in the late twenties with radiators piped to a boiler in the vestry. This proved to be inefficient and was later removed. Mains electricity was installed in 1934 – when it reached the village. The basic installation – free of charge of each dwelling, including the chapel, was just three lights and a single 5 amp 2-pin socket and plug. The lead covered cable used was then the norm.

When the vestry was built many appreciated the comfort and warmth of a fire. Preachers would often be invited for lunch by a trustee and usually stayed for the day. It was on these occasions that the preacher visited the Sunday School and gave a short talk to the children.

An attractive oak bracket with a heart feature attached was fashioned by father. It was fixed over the mantelshelf in the vestry and held a bust of John Wesley. When the chapel closed in 1981 it was given to me by the trustees; I restored it and it now hangs in my porch. I was also given the brass tablet erected in memory of James Arthur Tovey by his four sisters.

In time the opposition of earlier days was removed. A family of devout Christians lived at the Priory and took a generous and tolerant interest in the village life. James Tovey and his fellow Methodists held prayer meetings in the Priory drawing room. The Vicar of this period valued and respected their Christ-like sincerity; he was known to say to people who were 'under conviction' "I advise you to go to the Methodist Class Meetings". Truly a remarkable transformation.

I have a strong conviction for upholding Christian values, self-discipline and temperance. Sunday worship has always been paramount for a happy and fulfilling life and Wherwell for me has been very much a part of it.

above Interior of the Wesleyan Methodist Chapel showing part of the pulpit and communion rail with myself at the organ in 1975.
left Oak display bracket fashioned by father.

A colourful display of a Bible text (not seen now) which hung in my bedroom.

Threatened Demolition of the Chapel (1980s)

I am so pleased the chapel was not demolished. I fought hard to keep it as a dwelling and during the summer of 1982 I had correspondence with the Department of the Environment, London stating my case. The chapel was an unlisted building; application for listed building consent had been refused by the then Secretary of State.

I attended the inquiry at the Guildhall and was with an official from Hampshire County Council, who like me spoke in favour to retain it for conversion to a dwelling. After the meeting I was with the inspector at Wherwell to view its location. He agreed with me that demolition would aesthetically impair the character of the central area of the village – it would leave a gaping hole. Later the inspector upheld the decision and the chapel was saved. He said that a car park on the site would be an intrusive feature.

The plan for the site, which was backed by Test Valley Borough Council and the then Council Leader was for the chapel to be demolished and a car park put in its place. That, however, would not have solved the parking problem in Wherwell as it was much too small.

On closure of the Wesleyan Chapel this cellar was found underneath the building – the person seated is the Circuit Steward's wife.

Primitive Methodist Chapel

Wherwell was very much a Christian community and some 40 years after the Wesleyan chapel was built there was a desire to build another. It was the Primitive Methodist Chapel built on high ground at the south end of the 'Larches' in Fullerton Road. The 'Larches' was the home of the Spratt family and was built by Albert Spratt (senior). The new chapel was sited at the extreme end of his land, amidst a small plantation of larch trees, where it was narrow and of little value. Many remained after the chapel was built, and in my mind I can still see them there waving in a summer breeze through the coloured windows of the chapel. It is quite possible then that Albert Spratt provided the ground without charge and built the chapel.

The new chapel was a substantial brick-built building accessed by a rather steep flight of steps. A small utility room was added to the rear. Unlike the tall arched windows of the Wesleyan chapel the side windows were almost square with coloured panels. The roof space was left open, no doubt as a cost saving decision. To add a ceiling of that area would have been costly and, probably for the same reason, a porch was never built.

The entrance steps to the chapel were formed of chequered pattern Blue Staffordshire type bricks, with ordinary wall bricks for the side walls. At the roadside entrance was a pair of iron gates with an iron formed archway, attached to it was a framework to mount an oil lamp. Necessary in those days, steps could be so dangerous in the dark, especially for older people.

The chapel opened in 1888 at a cost of £350 – quite a substantial figure for those days. Already £200 had been raised, leaving only £150 to be paid, which they borrowed at 4% creating an annual charge of £6. However, not content with this and as a means of raising money, several of the lady members of the congregation were kept busy making clothing and other items for sale; toys, ornaments and other items were contributed by friends.

The first sale was held on Wednesday, 13 June 1888 at which the opening ceremony was performed by the Mayoress of Andover, followed by a short religious service conducted by the minister. Stalls were arranged down one side of the building, with lines carried across in order to display all the articles. On the opposite side a long table was laid out for tea. There were six ladies in charge of the selling. So successful was the undertaking that a sum of £10 was raised – a large sum in those days. No doubt there were many more sales to follow. One must admire the ingenuity, skill and enterprise of those devoted people.

The Primitive Methodists were a revivalist group founded in 1812 and were very influential among working class movements. The chapels were built by the pence of the poor as happened in Wherwell. Sunday services were at 3.00 pm and 6.00 pm. (There was no Sunday School.) Some members would attend the Wesleyan Chapel for morning service and many children attended the Wesleyan Sunday School. Coffee suppers would be provided for special occasions – always an attraction. The Chapel attracted people from Cottonworth and Fullerton.

We attended on special occasions – such as Harvest Festival. The harmonium was played by Elsie Monk who lived in one of the nearby cottages on the bankside.

Arranged by its members, camp meetings were held on the Common, usually twice a year. The chapel harmonium was carried across the Longbridge, usually by Mr Hand and Mr Hams, to the site further on.

A carrying handle at each end made this possible. Music was also provided by a concertina and two brass cornets. This lively ringing tone attracted walkers to the meeting.

A large number of people would gather there, including me, to enjoy the hearty singing and the music. Usually a visiting speaker from the circuit would address the meeting. Forms for seating were provided for the elderly. Children enjoyed running around in the wide open space. Camp meetings are mentioned in my poem 'Memories of a Favourite Walk'.

Wherwell Wesleyan Sunday School (1920s)

As I remember it there were four classes, two for boys and two for girls. At 2.30 pm a teacher would ring the school hand bell calling the children in.

Orderly good behaviour and attentiveness during class were paramount; sometimes the only voices heard were those of the teachers. One of my favourite hymns was:
"Lord, we thank Thee for the pleasure,
That our happy lifetime gives …."

As with day school, there were prizes to be won. For me it was a book with the title, 'Play Up, King's'.

During the springtime we would be rehearsing for the Sunday school anniversary – usually held in June. This would consist of singing, solos, readings and recitations – all done by the children and always to a full congregation. Music was provided by James Tovey playing the organ. This is the first verse of one of the songs – it had a bright and breezy tune.

The sun shines on the hilltop
It shines on hill and plain
It shines on barren deserts
And on the fruitful plain
For everyone, 'tis shining
'Tis shining bright and fair
For old and young, for rich and poor
The sun shines everywhere.

Some children were fortunate to have new clothes or shoes for the occasion. We were all dressed in our best; it was a happy day. But of course it was also for a purpose – the annual summer treat. I remember my first was an outing to Park Farm, it was by horse and cart – a four-wheeled farm wagon kindly provided by Mr Trowbridge at Manor Farm, from where we started. Imagine a cart load of excited, happy children, not really knowing where they were going – it was an adventure. I remember passing my home and proceeding along Longparish Road where we turned left to pass under the second railway arch. From there it was a bumpy ride along a winding track to the farm. Not a pleasant journey but fortunately no-one fell out.

Our venue was a quiet open grassland area surrounded by trees – from which scaffold ropes (probably from father) were slung from branches to provide us with swings. Arranged by the teachers we enjoyed a programme of games and races (no prizes I remember), after which it was time for tea. Seated on forms (in the open) at trestle-tables we enjoyed delicious bread and butter, dough cakes and much more from my grandparents' bakehouse and shop. (Many children then ate margarine.) After tea we were ready for another stop on the way home and arrived back at Manor Farm at 6.00 pm.

The following year we were by the riverside, privileged to use Mrs Holdaway's meadow in Fullerton Road. Increased numbers now attending Sunday school added to the excitement and more games were included in the programme, with the hilarious sack race and three legged race.

'Silver Queen' charabanc on one of its Sunday school annual outings.

In later years the summer treat was to the seaside by an open top 'Silver Queen' charabanc which was supplied by Mr Hiscock of Vernham Dean. It had a foldaway hood but I only remember it being used once. Boscombe was the first venue. Departing from the village at 7.30 am we arrived at the Pier head at about 10.30 am, having made a stop on the way. In the early twenties we had never seen the sea before, it was wonderful and so exciting with so much to do and enjoy. A splendid tea was provided for us at the Ashley Road Westleyan Methodist Church schoolroom. With another stop on the way home we arrived back at 9.00 pm.

Southsea and Swanage were also popular venues, but my favourite was Boscombe with its inspiring view descending the approach road to the Pier. Sadly it all too soon came to an end, the last outing was in 1930. Sometimes the return journey would be via Salisbury with a break of about 20 minutes.

Another special occasion was the annual Harvest Festival service celebrated at both morning and evening worship. The chapel would be tastefully decorated for this. Sheaves of corn provided by Mr Young were placed each end of the communion rail. The beautiful long bullrushes would be gathered by a waterkeeper and tastefully arranged. Vegetables and delicious fruit were in abundance. Mr Hand had a 'striped' variety apple tree – the delicious fruit would be placed in view of all because of

Happy seasiders at Boscombe.

Harvest Festival at the Wesleyan Methodist Chapel in the 1920s –
note the bracket mounted oil lamps either side of the pulpit.

its sweet smell. Hanging from the lamps either side of the pulpit would be a large bunch of black grapes – one could almost taste them. The Chapel, as with the village hall, was the centrepiece in those days.

The Sunday school anniversary did not provide sufficient funds to pay for the summer outings. In those days the ladies held a sewing class where they would be kept busy making things for the sale of work, which took place in the village hall. Various stalls displayed their wares which included needlework, fancy goods, millinery and jumble. Refreshments and tea were also provided. One year the proceeds amounted to over £13. I have no doubt that there were other contributions.

But that is not all for there was always a Christmas treat at the Iron Room. An excellent tea would be provided at 4.30 pm which commenced with Grace, sometimes said, sometimes sung. The first line was "Be present at our table Lord". Afterwards the tables were cleared away for games to commence; 'musical chairs' and 'musical mat' were always favourites, as was 'passing the parcel'. Punching balloons was also enjoyed. A great attraction was a beautifully laden Christmas tree lit by coloured candles and presents for all the children. The teachers also handed out crackers, an orange and a bag of sweets to each child on leaving the hall.

Interior of Wherwell Parish Church from an early 1920s postcard
showing the new electric lighting provided by The Priory.

It was the ladies' sewing class which generously gave of their time and money to help with the expenses. Mr Green, a great uncle of mine, was also thanked for the use of his car. He lived with his wife at Gavelacre, the long cottage close to the chapel. He purchased a new Austin Seven Tourer from Anna Valley Motors, Andover where I worked in the 1930s.

Chapter 10

Chilbolton

Village and Common

Approaching Chilbolton from Wherwell an old German field gun was sited in the Rectory meadow close to the school

In bygone days the Coronation Tree seat at the foot of West Down provided a spectacular view of the river below, across the water meadows and beyond. In summertime it was a popular resting place for Sunday evening walkers after taking the rising footpath from the Common.

From the 1920s – resting awhile at the Coronation Tree seat is Mrs Sturgess *(centre)* from Cottonworth Farm House with friends.

Water carts were popular with farmers for getting water to the cattle. Water would be hand-pumped from the rivulet stream which flows under the flat topped concrete bridge to the river, just a few yards beyond the entrance to the Common. The White House on the Common was the

The River Test, Chilbolton, 1951

From the roadside to the river-side, a delightful panoramic view with the Coronation Tree overlooking the River Test. (Reproduced by permission of the Frances Frith Collection)

former village Inn. Thomas Waterman was the publican, he was also a builder, carpenter and undertaker besides being a steeplejack – one notable steeple being on Salisbury Cathedral. Cricket was played nearby (ideal for rapid refreshment). In 1901 a silver watch and chain was won by Mr Golding of Cottonworth Farm House, Wherwell for the highest number of runs.

A horse-drawn farm water cart at the rivulet bridge – a second horse was required for the long climb back. Beyond it the former village Inn and cricket ground.

Tommy Baverstock was formerly the blacksmith at Chilbolton Village Forge before working for Mr Hand at Wherwell. He lived nearby at 'Horseshoe Cottage' next to the village shop. His mother was well-known and renowned for making her celebrated Easter wafering cakes from a closely guarded handed-down family recipe, using tongs in the baking process. Somewhat fragile the iron tongs suffered from breakage, but help was at hand – a dash to the forge by Tommy for a quick repair – all part of the blacksmith's craft.

The forge was somewhat small with space for only one horse. It was later demolished to make way for the New Inn construction – it was in the way.

The Mission Hall/Chapel

From memories of Chilbolton, passed on to me by father, brings to mind that at some time, possibly before or during the early part of the Great War, there was a Mission Hall in Cart Lane and that Mr Tibble was a preacher. But there were disadvantages for it in Cart Lane, it lacked impact in the village scene it was out of sight, out of mind and poorly attended.

Cart Lane was the approach to Mr Eastman's Farm and to the gated entrance to rising pasture land beyond. Much of the time it was wet and muddy as a result of rainfall draining down from the high ground, resulting in deep ruts formed by the heavy wheels of farm carts and wagons, especially when loaded. Dressed in one's Sunday best it is not surprising then that few people assembled there for worship.

Mr Tibble's solution to the problem was to relocate the Mission Hall to a more central village site – but where? He did not have to wait long to achieve his purpose.

Mrs Thomas Baverstock (wife of the village blacksmith) with two of her grandchildren at their Horseshoe Cottage home in 1933. *(courtesy of Henry Poore)*

Village Street looking south with attractive Test Cottage in the 1930s.
The turning on the left leads to Cart Lane and Poplar Farm. The New Inn sign can be seen in the distance.

As if providentially inspired, Mr Tibble acquired a plot of land from Mr Vearncombe, formerly the local Post and Telegraph Office. It was a prime central site for the Mission Hall/Chapel. However Mr Tibble also had another purpose for the land, it would provide him with a bungalow for his retirement and this was later built by father (see Chapter 6 – The Carpenter's Shop).

Brass lantern clock, a gift for father in the 1950s by the then owner of 'Test Cottage'.

Set back from the roadside by approximately 25 feet and close to Upcote Cottage a new site was prepared and concrete footings laid. Following this the timber constructed building in Cart Lane was dismantled and transported by horse and farm wagon and re-erected. For added appeal and improvement a porch was added with a gated pathway for access.

The chapel was now prominent in the village, it was a focal point and attracted full congregations. For Mr Tibble it was a dream come true. How fortunate he was to have a local preacher in the village to support him. Mr Ralph, living nearby, was a carter for Farmer Rose, he was well liked

Mid Village Street during the Great War, the Mission Hall/Chapel can be seen centre left. Extreme right with bicycle is Henry Olliff. (Before the arrival of the village shop and New Inn.)

and a popular preacher, always with a large congregation. (There is no doubt in my mind that Mr Ralph had much to do with the transportation of the building.)

The harmonium, a small reed organ with foot operated bellows, was played by Miss F Waterman and Miss Margaret Dunford. For some time there was an exceptionally large children's choir to provide hearty singing. The friendliness of those days and the teas on the chapel lawn were long remembered.

The chapel was cleaned by a young lady who lived opposite for sixpence a week.

As happened in Wherwell when the Wesleyan Methodist Chapel was built, it is quite possible that some resentment was expressed in Chilbolton with the re-siting of the Mission Hall/Chapel in the centre of the village, it was perceived to be unnecessary and perhaps obtrusive. Also because it was used for religious purposes it would not find favour with the Parish Church and perchance was considered a distracting influence.

Local Band

On Whit Monday in 1907 the newly formed brass band, comprising members from Wherwell, Chilbolton and Longparish assembled at Stocks Green beneath the village tree and played under the leadership of Mr Smith.

Stocks Green, Chilbolton, 1965

Stocks Green Triangle with its eye catching 'finger' signpost. Note the distinctive porch extension to Chilbolton Cottage. *(Reproduced by permission of the Francis Frith Collection)*

Church Fire

Much consternation was caused in the village on a Sunday morning in 1908 when it became known that the church was on fire. On arrival at the church at 6.00 pm to attend the fires which had been lit the night before, the Sexton found the pews at the west end on fire, the walls blackened and the church filled with dense smoke. The whole interior was much damaged. The fire was due to a fault in the hot air system. The gratings down the middle of the church are the remains of this discarded system.

The Rector would not have the church completely cleaned so that future generations could see the church had been on fire.

(Contributed by a former Chilbolton resident.)

In 1945 a disastrous fire in Village Street completely destroyed a pair of joined up thatched cottages which fronted the roadside adjoining the pathway to the Common. Living there at the time was the Voss family and Mrs Ralph.

The Village Street, Chilbolton, 1951

Village Street looking north, mid centre is Abbots Farm House, for many years home of the Dunford family. Lower left is where the two cottages were destroyed by fire. *(Reproduced by permission of the Francis Frith Collection)*

A De Bion Bouton car similar to that owned by Trevor Battye at Broxton Court. *(courtesy of Ken Braxton)*

Early Cars

In the very early years of the twentieth century cars began to appear in the village. Quite probably the first of the few was that of Trevor Battye of Broxton Court, a 12 miles per hour De Dion Bouton. The coachman who usually drove the horse drawn carriage was sent to Birmingham for a week to learn how to drive it. Petrol was then bought over the counter of the chemist's shop.

It took the family to Sunday morning church service and broke down in front of the whole congregation who gathered to see it. Jimmy Cole, a gardener at Broxton Court who lived in Broxton Cottages, was sent for to bring Jenny the donkey to tow the car home – a happy ending but what an embarrassment!

Mr Baylis of Chilbolton Manor House acquired a second-hand 1910 Clement Talbot five-seater car with a folding hood and detachable side screens in 1915. His two best riding horses, used in a trap, were commandeered by the Army during the Great War.

Major Turle of Digby Croft House acquired his first car in 1907, and in 1918 the Reverend Crowley of Chilbolton Rectory acquired a Model 'T' Ford.

A Clement Talbot car possibly owned by W Baylis at The Manor House, Chilbolton. *(courtesy of Ken Braxton)*

In superb condition, an early Model "T" Ford car similar to that acquired by the Rector at Chilbolton. (courtesy of C D L Brewett, Cornwall)

Land at Bargain Prices

About 1905 a Plan of Freehold land for sale by Mr C J Brake of Poplar House lists 272 plots of land for sale, at prices starting at £6. Among the cheapest was plot number 13, on the corner of Branksome Hill and Drove Lane, at £7.

The largest plot was number 1, later to be called Down End, at £373, while plot number 3, today's Test Rise, went for £128.

Chalkdell and the orchard opposite (formerly property of the late George Tilbury) was sold to Mr Henry Olliff in June 1906 for £610.

Bury Farm (St Michael's Cottage) estate, residence and buildings to Mr Hillier for £790. Also a pair of tenements at £75.

Winchester Way Field to Mr Rose (farmer) for £700. Twelve Acres Field and Garston to Mr Eastman (farmer) for £135. A dwelling house with shop, recently the local Post and Telegraph Office and cottage (opposite the present day shop), together with the Blacksmith and shop were sold to Mr Vearncombe for £160.

The Andover Advertiser, dated 19 July 1907, picked up on the Chilbolton development theme. "There are each year more visitors to this pretty spot during the summer months, and judging by the steady way in which plots for bungalows have been taken up and really substantial homes built on them Chilbolton will soon have a large number of residents who have elected to make their permanent home on its sunny down."

Mid Village, Chilbolton, 1951

Mid Village Street pictured later with shop development, circa 1960.
(Reproduced by permission of the Frances Frith Collection)

Bread Baking

Apart from wafering cakes, in the early part of the twentieth century a bakery business was set up by Percy Goodland around 1930 at his premises in Station Road where the family lived. Percy was assisted by his son Billie on leaving school when he was 14 – then the norm. In 1932 he acquired a new Morris Minor van for his delivery service, which included Wherwell, for at that time he supplied our daily bread.

Also living in Station Road was the well-known Pembroke family. They were members of the Christian Science Movement – which was much to do with faith healing, and held meetings in their house every Sunday evening at 8.00 pm. I remember my mother being invited to attend and I was there with her. Mr Pembroke was probably an enterprising gardener for I often saw him riding his bicycle in the village with a trug basket of produce over the handlebars.

Bread delivery round – the Goodland way. *(courtesy of Christine Wright)*

The Goodland family at their Chilbolton home in the early thirties.
from left Dorothea, Percy, Tommy and Billie. *(courtesy of Christine Wright)*

Relaxing at home in 1992 are (left to right) Tommy, Dorothea and Billie. *(courtesy of Christine Wright)*

Living next to the Pembroke family was George Duckett, not only was he headteacher at the village school and church organist (as previously mentioned), but also an agent for the Hampshire Friendly Society and attached to its Head Office in Jewry Street, Winchester. It was to Mr Duckett that I went for my Insurance Card when I started work.

Village Farmers

Mentioned earlier in my story, the much respected and hard working Dunford family lived at Abbots Farm in Village Street. Set back from the roadside, and a distinctive part of the village scene, was the large thatched barn in the farmyard. Adjoining it were the stables and a dairy. Robert (Bob) Dunford was a dairy farmer with a herd of nine cows and two horses, 'Topsy' and 'Spider' (horses then were much a part of the family). Two farm carts provided haulage for the farm. There were other livestock and of course chicken. Bob's elder son, Leslie, assisted and provided the daily milk round supplying their customers' needs. The large orchard, which bordered the opposite side of the road, was also owned by Bob Dunford. A prime central site, houses now occupy both areas.

This war-time aerial photograph of Chilbolton (mentioned earlier) pictures Abbots Farm with its grand old barn structure and orchard area. Lower centre is the bungalow built by father for Mr Tibble.

Another popular Chilbolton dairy farmer was Jack Eastman, also with a herd of nine cows and two horses, 'Boxer' and 'Flower', and two farm carts for haulage. He also kept chicken and probably much more. The family lived in a thatched cottage at the end of Cart Lane off Village Street. His dairy and farm buildings were close by. Using his bicycle, milk was delivered daily with two three-gallon hinged lid cans with a dipping measure slung over the handlebars – much the same as Rose Young did at Wherwell. Jack Eastman's cows, as with those of Bob Dunford, were pasture fed on the Common, producing pure, unpasteurised milk for good healthy living. Cream and fresh butter were a speciality. When it was time for the cows to return for milking, Jack Eastman would call them from the entrance gate to the Common – how well they knew him! When on my walks I often saw them in the river – which they had to cross to reach the pastures beyond.

Shoeing the horses for Jack Eastman and Bob Durnford was always done in their stables. Of course the sho'er was Tommy Baverstock, the Chilbolton blacksmith – he also made the new shoes.

Just a few yards from Bob Dunford, on the opposite side of Village Street, was another farmyard and another huge barn. The area extended northward from Cart Lane and extended to the roadside wall. The barn was at right angles and close to the road, with one corner just a few inches from the curvature area of the boundary wall, which made it a blind corner for motorists. The capped brick and flint wall along the road frontage gave it a pleasing appearance.

At its north end Eddy Wallis, the gamekeeper, lived in the cottage facing the barn. Apart from his game larder, he kept chicken and pigs in the farmyard.

Mr Rose and his family lived in a cottage there which fronted the road. Known as Farmer Rose, he was bailiff for Mr W Baylis at Chilbolton Manor. His daughter Mina attended the Andover Grammar School. The family later moved to a cottage on the opposite side of the road which was close to our yard. In later years the barn was dismantled by father – piece by piece, with just one of his workmen. The heavy oak timbers were moved across the road to our yard. The new Rectory now occupies the site.

Allotments

The footpath leading from Village Street to Joys Lane, a short cut to the Common, was not always so for the land within this area contained the village allotments and a private orchard. The orchard was owned by Mr Olliff who lived at Chalkdell. It was later acquired by Colonel Bush, living at St Michael's Cottage. However, development was inevitable and later it was used for housing.

Old Village Hall

The old village hall was constructed by C Grace and Sons, Building Contractors of Clatford at a cost of £310 in 1891 and took about five months to complete. The Dean of Winchester, the Very Reverend G W

Kitchen, DD and Mrs Silva of Testcombe laid the foundation stones for the building on 11 April 1891. Both were presented with the silver trowels used for that purpose. On 15 September the hall was officially opened. To mark the occasion approximately 100 children attended the opening and were later provided tea in a barn lent by Farmer Rose. For the 200 or more adults a grand tea was provided by Mr Olliff (from his shop and bakery at Wherwell) in the new hall, with a small bouquet on each plate – a souvenir keepsake. The silver trowel used by the Dean was later offered to and accepted by the Parish Council. A glass fronted display case for it was made by father and placed on the fireplace mantelshelf for all to see – until decades later it was broken into and the trowel stolen. However, it was later retrieved – a local man was the culprit!

Pictured in May 1986 the 95th anniversary of the building of Chilbolton's former village hall.
(courtesy of the Andover Advertiser)

It was some time later that a resident contacted me with the story adding "as your father had made it would you repair it?" This I did in my workshop. I also made a new key for the brass lock and added a keyhole escutcheon. To enhance its appearance I fitted a capped pitched roof section with a pole. For this I made and attached a small wooden trowel to give it an eye catching appeal. The hardwood moulded panel which I added below the case now holds an inscription plate. It is now located in the Durnford Room at the new hall.

The grindstone was sited in the grounds of the village hall until the hall was demolished.

My story of the villages of Wherwell and Chilbolton is a celebration of a rural environment and of the many wonderful people who through the years have touched upon my life. Though many have passed on I can still hear their voices, their laughter and see their smiling faces. I am grateful to have known them.

A pot plant presented to mother by Edie Vincent at Chilbolton village hall.

Silver trowel case – after restoration in my workshop.

My 'Shield of Honour' production. Badges displayed are School Prefect – Wendy; Women's Royal Air Force, Medical Insignia – my sister-in-law Kate; Andover Grammar School Medallion – Norman and Fay (my younger daughter); Royal Air Force Officer's Cap Badge (Norman).

Chapter 12

In Celebration

I have long enjoyed writing poetry. Many of my poems have been written to celebrate the events that have happened to me during my life and I have included these three for, hopefully, your enjoyment.

Snow on the Mount

Jingle Bells, Jingle Bells,
Jingle all the way,
O what fun it is to ride,
On a homemade wooden sleigh,
Jingle Bells, Jingle Bells,
Up the Lane we go,
High upon the Mount,
And in the deep, deep snow.
A wintry, snowy scene,
So peaceful and serene,
Happy voices everywhere,
I'm so glad that I was there,
On the fast-track run,
Ready for the start,
A push, we're off,
Get out the way,
And whoops we're down again.

The poem is a pastiche of the well-known Christmas song Jingle Bells and can be sung to the same tune.

The Blacksmith's Shop

A blacksmith's shop stood at the top of the hill,
A favourite place to gaze and thrill,
For the blacksmith had a special skill,
Pumping the bellows with cinders flying
Until the red hot iron was ready for plying,
A dash to the anvil with hammer and tongs,
Sparks flying everywhere in cascading throng.
The hammer bouncing off the anvil in rhythmic time
      and effortless ease,
That lovely solid ringing sound was magic in my ear,
Moving the horseshoe round the anvil's tapered shaft,
For that perfect shape, with hand and eye –
      the blacksmiths craft,
With fire and tongs and the water trough.

This next verse is special to me as it was composed by my late brother, Norman:

When the hammer rang the anvil,
And the sparks flew 'cross the floor,
Children raced from all directions,
To the smithy's open door,
Clear off! Clear off! old Tommy would shout,
Before I have to kick you out!
And as for you, young Percy Trodd,
Can't you see I have a horse to be shod?

The verses were written in celebration of a craft long-lost from so many villages.

Memories of a Favourite Walk
(in Wherwell and Chilbolton in the 1920s and 1930s)

Away from 'Mount View' and up the lane,
Across the Fairpiece was less of a strain,
The beautiful beech trees across the top ridge,
Where I remember I sat on the grass with my class for a drawing lesson,
Playing cricket was a popular game until the ball rolled down the line,
"Yer tis" someone yelled, but too late again, it was time to end the session.

Crossing the old hill with cobbler Monk nearby, our boots and shoes did mend,
Passing the school and the narrow footpath, onto the road and hairpin bend,
Across 'Above Town' with the clump beyond,
Looking over the railway and the village below,
Always quite sure to make your heart glow.

Resting awhile on a large tree root,
The wind whistling gently through the trees so tall,
Enjoying the scene and the magnificent view with inspiring awe,
Dropping down to the railway and over the line,
"Stop, Look and Listen" read the Notice, there could be a train on the "Nile" to make us smile.

Down to Longbridge, a pause to gaze at the river below,
Over the Common, where people loved to stroll, in our
Sunday best with a cheery hello,
The little white chalk humps to guide the way,
Where camp meetings were held and the band would play.

Across the Chilbolton end bridge and onto the right,
A shady little path by a little stream, climbing to the
    seat at the foot of the Down,
A wide open view of the river and meadows, what a
    delightful sight,
Enjoyed by so many, a favourite trysting place,
For everything was at a leisurely pace.

Or:

Leaving the Common and into the lane,
Wet and muddy, it was always the same,
Down through the village, past Hunt's little shop,
Just a wooden hut I remember, but a prime central spot.

On to Frog Lane and over the stile,
Passing the church and school, then across the
    meadows,
The little stream where we went to paddle,
Not far away the cowslips we loved to gather.

Across big bridge, then Scott's little lodge, the
    waterkeeper,
To Winchester corner and home for a breather.